HARRIET HOSMER • LOST AND FOUND

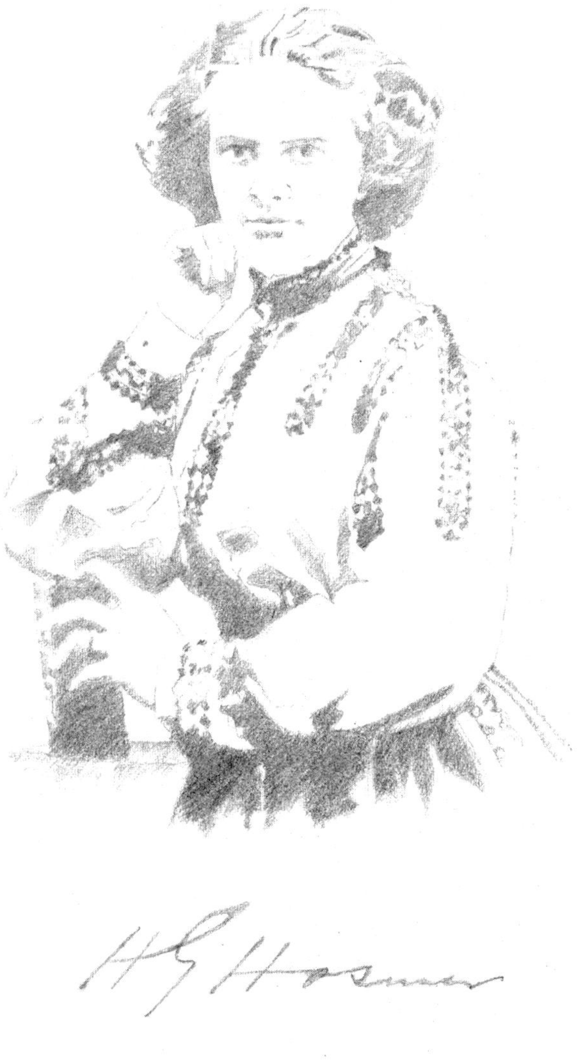
H G Hosmer

PATRICIA CRONIN

HARRIET HOSMER
LOST AND FOUND
A
CATALOGUE RAISONNÉ

CHARTA

Design
Daniela Meda, Gabriele Nason

Editorial Coordination
Filomena Moscatelli

Copyediting
Emily Ligniti

Copywriting and Press Office
Silvia Palombi Arte&Mostre, Milano

US Editorial Director
Francesca Sorace

Promotion and Web
Monica D'Emidio

Distribution
Antonia De Besi

Administration
Grazia De Giosa

Warehouse and Outlet
Roberto Curiale

Cover
Medusa, 2006

Page 2
Frontispiece, 2007

Page 3
Title Page, 2007

ISBN 978-88-8158-732-2

Printed in Italy

Edizioni Charta srl
Milano
via della Moscova, 27 - 20121
Tel. +39-026598098/026598200
Fax +39-026598577
e-mail: charta@chartaartbooks.it

Charta Books Ltd.
New York City
Tribeca Office
Tel. +1-313-406-8468
e-mail: international@chartaartbooks.it

www.chartaartbooks.it

Acknowledgements

This project was encouraged, nurtured, and supported by many people and institutions along the way. The Schlesinger Library, Radcliffe College, Harvard University, and Watertown Free Public Library have fascinating Hosmer Archives and were incredibly helpful. The National Library of Scotland was also generous with Lady Ashburton's Archive in Edinburgh, Scotland.

Generous financial support came from the Louis Comfort Tiffany Foundation, New York Foundation for the Arts, Deutsche Bank, the PSC-CUNY grant from the Research Foundation of The City University of New York and Scholar Incentive Award from Brooklyn College.

The American Academy in Rome awarded me the John Armstrong Chaloner/Jacob H. Lazarus – Metropolitan Museum of Art Rome Prize in Visual Art, which provided me a transformative year retracing Hosmer's career in Rome. Heartfelt thanks to President Adele Chatfield-Taylor and Director Carmela V. Franklin for their gracious guidance and for being inspiring role models. Thank you also to Mellon Professor Thomas McGinn for the informative walking tours and the trip to Sicily that changed my perspective.

Heiskell Arts Director, Dana Prescott, the unofficial cultural ambassador of Italy, is not only my lifestyle guru, but also one of my most stalwart supporters. She introduced me to many wonderful people and Italian cities. I am so grateful for her friendship.

Heartfelt thanks go to John Guare for his inspired reading of Hosmer's "Doleful Ditty" in Caffè Greco. Thank you to AAR Trustee Michael Conforti for climbing up to get Hosmer's inscription on her *Tomb of Judith Falconnet* in Sant'Andrea della Fratte Church. Deep appreciation goes to Resident Phoebe Dent Weil for her boundless enthusiasm and continued support of this project. Thank you to Mona Talbott, another lifestyle guru who, in my humble opinion, just might save the world.

Thank you to all the 2006–2007 Rome Prize Fellows, Fellow Travelers, Residents, Visiting Artists, and Scholars for their creative and intellectual stimulation. Big shout outs especially to: Tom Bissell, John Kelly, Dave King, Christopher MacEvitt, Marina Rustow, Thomas Tsang, and Gregory Waldrop for their friendship, solace, eye-opening travels, and late night hi-jinx that are too numerous and/or embarrassing to list here. Additional thanks to Tiffany Abernathy, Andrea Barnet, Martha Pollak, Lisa Mignone, Andrew Norman, Arman Schwartz, James Graham Turner, and Kit White.

Thank you to Carole Biagiotti for exhibiting this work at Galleria Biagiotti Progetti Arte, in Florence, and for cheering me on. Grazie mille to Susan Sanders and Laura Flushe, the dynamic duo behind The Institute of Design + Culture in Rome and eternallycool.net for their friendship, generosity, and the best roof-top dinner parties in Rome.

Special thanks to Julia Markus for her brilliant book, *Across an Untried Sea: Discovering Lives Hidden in the Shadow of Convention and Time* about Charlotte Cushman and her circle of expatriate women in Rome. It truly inspired me.

To Maura Reilly, the founding curator of the Elizabeth A. Sackler Center for Feminist Art at the Brooklyn Museum, my eternal gratitude for her vision to bring this project to the attention of Charta Art Books and the Brooklyn Museum. This book and the exhibition at the Brooklyn Museum would not exist without you. Thank you to Lauren Ross at the Brooklyn Museum for seeing what Maura saw.

Thank you to William H. Gerdts for his superb essay in this book and also for generously opening up his home and Hosmer files to me.

This book is made possible by the support of Sara Vance and Michelle Waddell. Their friendship and belief in my work has been sustaining. And to A.G. Rosen and Debi Sonzogni who have been there for me since the beginning. They bought the first piece of art I ever sold and continue to be great friends and traveling companions. Thank you to Brooks Adams and Lisa Leibmann for their assistance and encouragement and Liz Christensen, curator of Deutsche Bank.

For Filomena Moscatelli, Francesca Sorace, and Giuseppe Liverani at Edizioni Charta, Milan and New York, sincere appreciation for making my dream a reality.

Thank you to Colleen Asper for her talent, diligence, and Internet sleuthing, Ray Henders at Rayographix for his excellent work, and Lois Plehn for her constant encouragement. Deep appreciation for their patience, humor, and years of conversation, song, and dance: Janet Biggs and Bob Cmar, Michael Plante, Thom Collins and Matt Goodrich. You have aided in the progress of my work more than you know.

I was so happy that most of my family, dubbed the Cronini, was able to visit me for a week in Rome. Their belief in me has been a source of great strength. And to Robert Rosenblum, I owe a debt that can never be repaid, for giving me the confidence to write this book.

And finally, to my greatest love, Deborah Kass, my deep gratitude for letting me move to Rome for a year and get my mojo back. She taught me everything I know about thinking outside the box and gave me the courage to act on it. This book is dedicated to her.

Contents

Preface

Maura Reilly

Harriet Hosmer: Lost and Found, A Catalogue Raisonné by Patricia Cronin is an interventionist project that calls special attention to work by women as cultural producers—Cronin's as well as that of Harriet Hosmer. This conceptually complex catalogue raisonné and related exhibitions challenge the broader framework of art history and its exhibition practices for being unconditionally masculinist. In other words, it takes as its operative assumption that the art system—its institutions, his-stories, and so forth—is a hegemonic discourse that privileges "white male creativity to the exclusion of all women artists."[1] As a counter-hegemonic project, then, Cronin's Hosmer catalogue raisonné and related exhibitions expand the canons of art history to include what it had hitherto refused—women, and lesbians, in particular. It can be understood, then, as a corrective to the omission of women and feminists from the art-historical records, past and present.

Cronin came to the subject of Hosmer somewhat fortuitously. While researching her marble mortuary sculpture *Memorial To A Marriage* (2002) for art historical precedents she stumbled upon a sepulcher by Hosmer called the *Tomb of Judith Falconnet* (1857–1858) that stunned her; the quality of execution was superb, the neo-classical style on a par with Antonio Canova, she believed. Who was this artist, she wondered? And, as someone who had studied the history of sculpture extensively, why had she never heard of her? It was at that moment that she decided Hosmer was to be her next project.

In 2003, Cronin began researching the biography and oeuvre of Hosmer. The more she learned about the artist, her work, and of her international fame during her lifetime, the more astonished Cronin was by the dearth of scholarly material. Why had this artist been obscured by art history? By extension, if not remembered for her artwork then why not for her notorious reputation and delicious biography? As the leader of the White Marmorean Flock in Rome—as it was so dubbed by Henry James—who surrounded herself with a circle of emancipated women, included among them actress Charlotte Cushman and sculptor Edmonia Lewis, but also by such esteemed literary figures as Nathaniel Hawthorne and Elizabeth Barrett Browning, the American-born Hosmer was a notorious lesbian with aristocratic lovers, as well as a self-supporting artist with international clients and highly regarded sculptural commissions. Her biography was the stuff of great nineteenth-century novels. Yet there has been nothing substantive written about Hosmer, her life or work—that is, until now.

In *Harriet Hosmer: Lost and Found* Cronin plays biographer, art historian, and artist, in an effort to offer the first comprehensive catalogue raisonné dedicated exclusively to an extraordinary nineteenth-century woman artist, Harriet Hosmer. As biographer and art historian, Cronin fastidiously researched every work produced by Hosmer, from her first original sculpture of 1852 to her last in 1893. This thorough study offers locations of works, provenance, and exhibitions histories and detailed, formal analyses written in a fresh, contemporary style. The sheer breadth of information contained herein is extraordinary and represents a truly heroic feat, especially considering that

Cronin was starting from scratch. Also included is an extraordinary essay by art historian, William H. Gerdts, who is a leading expert on the White Marmorean Flock. In sum, the catalogue will certainly remain for years to come the definitive scholarly text on Hosmer.

Art historian is only one role that Cronin plays in this multi-layered counter-hegemonic project—the most complex being that of artist. How should she re-produce Hosmer's sculptural work in the catalogue, most of which is not locatable, no longer extant, only known via descriptions or via old photographs? How to reclaim and insert into the canon the life's work of a nearly forgotten artist? While it would have been fairly simple for Cronin to reproduce the surviving works by Hosmer in digital format, she opted instead to present artistic interpretations of the sculptures in small, unique monochrome watercolors—Cronin's preferred medium and because she believed it best represented the luminosity of marble. Each of Hosmer's catalogue entries, then, is accompanied by a reproduction of a watercolor, by Cronin, that depicts a sculpture, by Hosmer. (In the cases where the work no longer exists, as in Hosmer's famous *Queen of Naples* [1868], Cronin has produced a ghost image.)

Issues surrounding postmodern appropriation, and critiques of authorship and aura, are therefore central to Cronin's Hosmer project. These ideas are not new to Cronin, though. Her most famous work to-date, *Memorial To A Marriage*, discussed above, pays direct homage to nineteenth-century realist painter, Gustave Courbet, by appropriating his infamous 1866 lesbian painting, *The Sleepers*, as its formal source. This usurption of a male modern master's language as her own is a tactical mime that functions effectively to deconstruct modernist myths of originality and authorship.

On the contrary, in choosing a female artist, one who was famous in her day yet relatively unknown today, Cronin's deconstructivist project diverges from her previous interventionist project, *Memorial To A Marriage*. With the Hosmer project she is highlighting instead the canon of art history's exclusions and inclusions, thereby figuring forth its discriminatory practices and sexist foundations that make it acceptable for certain artists—male—to be raised to the canon's heights and others not.

It is during her final role, that of curator, that Cronin's project completes itself. Scholarly catalogue raisonné and correlating watercolors in hand, Cronin-as-curator can now present her and Hosmer's work for exhibitions. The first public unveiling of the project took place at The American Academy in Rome, in 2007, where Cronin had been a fellow working on the Hosmer project. It was a most apt and historically ironic location, considering Hosmer's lifelong relationship to Rome but also the fact that throughout the nineteenth century in Rome women artists were prohibited from taking courses at the art academies. The exhibition was suggestively titled *An American in Rome*, leaving viewers to wonder whom the American was, Cronin or Hosmer? Forty of a total of sixty-two watercolors were exhibited, hung simply with pins to the wall, and no explanatory wall texts. Thusly placed, outside the context of the catalogue raisonné, the objects now become a museological intervention in the lineage of other "minority" artists such as Fred Wilson, Kara Walker, or Zoe Leonard who have all produced "interventions" that are meant to challenge the race and/or sex biases of institutions.

In 2009, the project will have its U.S. debut at the Elizabeth A. Sackler Center for Feminist Art at the Brooklyn Museum, where it will be featured in The Herstory Gallery, an exhibition space that is meant to work in conceptual tandem with Judy Chicago's *The Dinner Party* (1974–1979), a monumental feminist installation that commemorates 1,038 female figures. In proximity to an iconic work famous for its strategies of reclamation (historical, women's work, vaginal iconology), Cronin's project will shine and glory in the feminist context that is its conceptual lineage. Thusly located, it will also remind us what art historian Linda Nochlin proclaimed decades ago, when she insisted that the feminist project of the 1970s needed to start with the unburying and resurrection of women from history before analysis and deconstruction of the canon could commence.[2] Cronin's *Harriet Hosmer: Lost and Found, A Catalogue Raisonné* has proven that Nochlin's rallying cry has in part been answered. It also functions as a reminder that there are many more women artists to be discovered, unearthed, and displayed on museum walls and pedestals.

1. Griselda Pollock, *Differencing the Canon: Feminist Desire and the Writing of Art Histories*. London and New York: Routledge, 1999, p. 10.
2. Linda Nochlin, "Why Have There Been No Great Women Artists?," in *Women, Art and Power and Other Essays*. New York: Harper & Row, 1988, pp. 145–178.

Lost and Found

Patricia Cronin

"Nothing provokes meditation more than absence."
Brian Stock[1]

In 2000 I received a large grant from the Kansas City, Missouri based foundation, Grand Arts, to make my dream piece—a 3 ton marble over life-size mortuary statue titled *Memorial To A Marriage* of my partner, the artist Deborah Kass, and myself, destined for our burial plot in Woodlawn Cemetery in the Bronx, designed in 1863 as America's Pere La Chase.

I began researching the history of sculpture in order to make mine. The history of sculpture is dominated by death, burials, and memorials. In fact, the history of sculpture IS the history of death. While combing through every tome on sculpture, I stumbled across two statues I had never seen before. They were extraordinary. One was of Beatrice Cenci and the other was the Tomb of Judith Falconnet. I fell in love. I looked at the artist's name below each reproduction and read the words "Harriet Hosmer." I said out loud, "Hmmm, I've never heard of her." And then wondered, "WHY had I never heard of her?" I knew then and there she would be my next project. While I was thinking about my own death when creating *Memorial To A Marriage*, I found someone else's life.

Harriet Hosmer (1830–1908) moved to Rome in 1852 when she was twenty-two years old, apprenticed with the leading neo-classical sculptor, British artist John Gibson, and very quickly hung out her own shingle and became known as the first professional woman sculptor. Hosmer lived within a lively Anglo-American expatriate community of writers and artists, as well as a circle of "independent women." In her time, she had a prominent career, was critically acclaimed, financially successful, and exhibited in all the international exhibitions. She was infamous. Today, her works are in the best museum collections in the world and yet she is largely unknown.

Who gets written into history? Who is forgotten? Why, how, and what are the conditions in which eradication can occur? How is value determined? These elements coalesce at the intersection of the ivory tower and the art market that is the catalogue raisonné.

My Hosmer Catalogue Raisonné is made by hand. Each of her neo-classical marble statues is represented by a monochromatic watercolor. Because of its transparent properties, watercolor is the perfect medium to represent the luminosity of marble—how light penetrates the surface of marble, swirls around about an inch below the surface before it bounces back out. The watercolor images of Hosmer's statues are arranged in chronological order and are interspersed with ghost images of statues that have been unlocatable to-date, including one that the *London Art Journal* (the *Artforum* of its day) called Hosmer's crowning achievement: her masterpiece the life-size marble statue of the last Queen of Naples. Although there are contradicting written descriptions, there is no visual documentation of Hosmer's *Queen of Naples*. How to visually represent something I cannot see has been a question I've been grappling with for some time.

Living in Rome for a year, tracing Hosmer's footsteps, surrounded by Catholicism, majestic churches, mysticism, stories of miracles and saints' lives has helped me shape the answer: an apparition, a phantom for missing statues, and a lost career.

1. Medieval historian Brian Stock in a conversation with the artist in her studio at the American Academy in Rome on February 25, 2007.

The Leader of The Flock

William H. Gerdts

Though sculptural works were produced in this country even during the Colonial period—gravestones, weathervanes, ships' figureheads—monumental figural pieces primarily created in the near-sanctified medium of marble were exceedingly few, and all were produced by British artists, including some public monuments and a number of church memorials. After the American Revolution, a number of Italian carvers came to this country, both to produce likenesses of America's leading military and political leaders and to decorate public buildings, churches, and especially the United States Capitol, while several native artists also undertook to produce marble sculptures, again, primarily portraits. But the first "school" of American sculpture may be said to have begun in 1825, when the Boston artist, Horatio Greenough, traveled to Europe to begin a successful career abroad—one of several men who have had passed on to them the designation of "The Father of American Sculpture."

Following his return to Boston after an illness which he contracted in Rome, Greenough returned and settled in Florence, and for the next two generations of American sculptors, almost all those who achieved any degree of celebrity and prominence worked in Florence or Rome, the latter becoming more and more the destination of choice. There they studied ancient and contemporary work, located the workmen who did the actual carving of the sculptures that they modeled in clay, found themselves in proximity to the marble quarries from which they drew their material, and joined a community of artists which included some American painters, but more significantly, an international tribe of professional sculptors from all over Europe. These artists, American and European, were all working within variations of the dominant neo-classic aesthetic determined by simplified form, harmonious proportions, and idealized subject-matter, an approach to sculpture inaugurated at the end of the eighteenth century by Antonio Canova and continued by the Danish artist Bertel Thorwaldsen, still active when Americans first joined their European confreres in Italy. While some of the Americans sent work back to America for exhibition—two versions of Hiram Powers's most famous sculpture, *The Greek Slave*, toured the United States, city by city, in the later 1840s and early 1850s, and a good many major sculptures by Americans and Europeans began to appear in the International Exhibitions (the Worlds' Fairs) which were inaugurated in 1851, the majority of commissions for the Americans came from their fellow citizens visiting Italy while making the Grand Tour of Europe. (It should be noted, though, that American patrons also did acquire sculptures by Europeans, while a number of English collectors became patrons of a few of the Americans: Hiram Powers, William Wetmore Story, and Harriet Hosmer.) Guidebooks were published giving not only the addresses of the sculptors but also featuring descriptions of their latest accomplishments. Well-to-do American patrons would visit the sculptors' studios to have their portraits created and to look over the artists' ideal plasters of classical, religious, allegorical, and literary subjects, often choosing one or more for marble replication. In turn, these works, once on private display after their prolonged delivery back home, often might inspire their friends and neighbors to order replications, even without going abroad to visit the studios and the sculptors. Some of these American sculptors stayed in Italy for a few years and returned home, but most of them spent their entire careers abroad, and a good many died in Italy where their families are buried in what Henry James described as "the most beautiful thing in Italy" and the "sweetest sanctity in all Rome"—the Protestant Cemetery.

James was as or even more familiar with Italy than he was with France and England, both of which served as his home for most of his career, and certainly more than the United States, which he visited often but which was never his residence. He was extremely familiar with the American sculptors in Rome, and included among his prolific writings was his two-volume account of *William Wetmore Story and His Friends*, published in Boston in 1903. It was a letter of 1853 from Story to James, concerning Harriet Hosmer, which later inspired the great writer to identify her as "the most eminent member of that strange sisterhood of American 'lady sculptors' who at one time settled upon the seven hills in a white, marmorean flock." James's further remarks on the women sculptors to whom he referred are gently and not unkindly patronizing, and recent scholars have derided his commentary, not unjustly, as likening these women to either birds or sheep, both communally categorized as "flock." (James almost surely was referring to birds rather than sheep, for birds "settle" on hills; sheep "roam" them.) And yet James's comments also hint to some degree of admiration, in part for the diversity within the uniqueness of these women, and as likened to birds, high-flying and independent. At the same time he particularly returned to Hosmer, admired perhaps more for her "character, strong, fresh and interesting," but also acknowledged for her talent. What had obviously struck James as it did a good many other observers were the number of American women sculptors who congregated in Italy over a short period of time in the mid-nineteenth century: Hosmer in 1852, Louisa Lander in 1855, Emma Stebbins in 1856, Florence Freeman in 1861, Margaret Foley in 1862, Edmonia Lewis in 1865 and Blanche Nevin about the same time, Anne Whitney in 1867, and Vinnie Ream in 1869.

Hosmer was one of the earliest of the significant group of American women sculptors to settle in Rome, preceded only by Boston's Sarah Fisher Clampitt Ames, who journeyed there in the mid-1840s, after marrying the portraitist, Joseph Ames, but she did not remain to become part of the "flock." In any case, Hosmer was hardly the first professional woman sculptor. As early as the thirteenth century, Sabina von Steinbach is recorded as working with her father, Erwin von Steinbach, on the sculptural decorations of the Cathedral of Strasbourg, while in the seventeenth century, Louisa Roldan achieved considerable reputation in Spain. A forebear to the Americans such as Hosmer was the English sculptor, Anne Seymour Damer, an early neo-classicist of the later eighteenth century; one of her British teachers was Giuseppe Ceracchi who later became the most distinguished sculptor in the new United States in the last decade of the century. France produced a number of highly talented and well respected women sculptors in the nineteenth century, some contemporary with the "white marmorean flock," such as Felicie de Fauveau, working in Florence, and Susan Durant, the mid-nineteenth-century English sculptor of considerable talent, even exhibited a bust of Harriet Beecher Stowe at London's Royal Academy in 1857. Much earlier in colonial America, Patience Lovell Wright was the best-known of a number of women sculptors who modeled portraits in wax, moving from New York to England just before the Revolution, during which time she also served as a spy for the Americans! Before the middle of the century, the only woman sculptor of any note working to create life-size imagery in the United States, forgoing European experience, was the semi-professional Joanna Quiner of Salem and Boston, though she appears to have worked only in plaster. The English sculptor, Horatia Augusta Latilla Freeman, was married to the American painter, James Freeman, and lived in Rome where she was active as a sculptor from the mid-1850s on. However, she does not seem to have had significant association with the band of American women under discussion here, though she appears to have been distantly related to the unmarried American sculptor from Boston, Florence Freeman, almost an exact contemporary, who was one of the less well-known of the "flock."

What is known about Freeman is that she went to Italy with the great actress, Charlotte Cushman, in 1861, following the path that Harriet Hosmer had taken nine years earlier; in fact, though originally settled in Florence, under Hosmer's influence Freeman relocated to Rome the following year. The degree of Hosmer's impact upon her women colleagues in Rome, both in terms of their personal relationships and in the thematic artistic choices they made, is difficult to discern, but that Hosmer was the leading figure of the "flock" and the only one to achieve truly international recognition there is no question. Born in Watertown, Massachusetts, she attended Mrs. Charles (Elizabeth) Sedgwick's very progressive school in Lenox in that state, and having decided to pursue the study of sculpture even in her youth, she took lessons with the able but today little-known sculptor, Peter Stephenson, in Boston in late 1849. One key to Hosmer's superiority over many of her female contemporaries lay in her study in 1850–1851 with Dr. Joseph N. McDowell at the Medical College in St. Louis, since women artists, painters, or sculptors otherwise had no recourse to anatomical training. McDowell was persuaded to allow Hosmer to attend his lectures by his good friend, Wayman Crow, the father of one of Hosmer's schoolmates; Hosmer created a portrait medallion of McDowell in 1851, and much later, in 1865, she was to carve a bust of Crow who was visiting Rome at the time. Crow, in turn, became one of the four most influential figures in Hosmer's career, along with Charlotte Cushman, John Gibson, and Louisa, Lady Ashburton. It was in 1852 that Hosmer sailed to Italy at Cushman's urging, where she settled in Rome and where Cushman presided over an ever-increasing group of American women, including a good number of sculptors. Cushman's artistic entourage was not entirely female; the American, Paul Akers, and the English sculptor, Shakespeare Wood, were also in her set, though others, such as Randolph Rogers, were openly contemptuous. Cushman herself had excelled theatrically not only in female characters, but also in male roles such as Romeo and Hamlet. It would be erroneous either to associate all the American women sculptors in Rome with Cushman's circle, just as it would be a mistake to identify their association in all cases as lesbian. Indeed, one of the "flock," Louisa Lander, hitherto patronized by Nathaniel Hawthorne, was censured and in a sense "expelled" from the expatriate artistic community for what remains a mysterious heterosexual sexual offence. On the other hand, the lesbian identification of at least some of these artists must certainly account, to some degree, for their preference for strong-minded, independent women within their artistic repertory.

Excluding the slightly earlier Sarah Ames, the question must be addressed as to what brought this rather considerable number of American women sculptors to congregate and develop their professional skills in Rome in this relatively brief period, some admittedly for a longer period of time and/or more successfully than others. The explanation, I believe, is complex. Charlotte Cushman's position as a guiding mentor, even if not all the women developed a connection with her, was vital to this development, as was her homoerotic preferences, again even if these were shared by only a segment of the "flock." In any case, Cushman's sexual preferences were echoed by Margaret Foley's close relationship with the English sculptor, Elizabeth Hadwin, while Anne Whitney lived her life with Adeline Manning, a painter who had studied in France with Thomas Couture. Italy, perhaps Rome and the Vatican even more than most Italian cities, would not have been any more receptive or even tolerant of aberrant behavior than would their native American habitats. But their identification with the arts and especially sculpture provided them with a cloak of curiousness that characterized them and their often eccentric conduct—unescorted or solely female-dependent, quasi-male costuming and the like—more bizarre than condemned. But an important addition to this mix for at least limited acceptability was their nationality; contemporary records locate a few French and British professional woman sculptors active in Italy at the time (along with Jane Morgan, from Ireland) but no Italians. And when these women did mix, both professionally and socially outside their own company, it was invariably with English-speaking male colleagues and their families; American and English writers such as the Hawthornes and the Brownings; and with patrons from both Britain and America. In other words, they remained as foreign in Italy as they would have appeared, in a different sense, as "foreign" or outlandish, back in the United States. And one might reverse this argument, also, and suggest that one of the main reasons these women settled in Rome was that the prohibitions and inhibitions still current in American social and sculptural life in the 1850s and 1860s prompted them to seek out a foreign environment which might allow them greater freedom of lifestyle.

Even before leaving America and traveling to Italy, Hosmer had carved a sculptural bust of *Hesper*, the evening star, one of a number of subjects that the women sculptors derived from the poetry of Alfred, Lord Tennyson, in this case, his poem, "In Memoriam," which begins with the words "Sad Hesper . . ." The sculpture served her well, for once in Rome she was able to convince the resident English artist, John Gibson, to take her on as a pupil; Gibson was considered at the time one of the greatest, if not the greatest, sculptor working in Italy. The connection she established with Gibson proved invaluable to Hosmer, not only in the superb training she received, which was crucial to her evolution as one of the finest of the neo-classic sculptors in Italy, but, working out of the master's studio for six years until she secured her own, Hosmer also attracted a clientele that was fully as British as it was American. Ultimately, of course, it was this very connection which led to Hosmer's near-abandonment of her chosen field after disillusionment with post-unification Italy, living much of her later life in England. Many of her later years were spent at Melchet Court in Hampshire, England, the country home of Louisa, Lady Ashburton, both patron and lover, and at Kent House, the town house that Lady Ashburton built in London between 1872 and 1874, often with the advice of Hosmer and Lady Marianne Alford, their mutual friend and another of Hosmer's major English patrons. In addition, Lady Ashburton provided Hosmer with a studio in Albert Gate Studios nearby on William Street in London.

A detailed review of Hosmer's artistic achievement is beyond the scope of this essay, and is, in any case, contained within the catalogue raisonné. Superficially, it might appear not too different from those of her contemporaries, male and female. Some of these artists such as Hiram Powers created far more portrait busts than they did what are termed "ideal" works—i.e., subjects drawn from literature, the classical world, allegory, religion, or the imagination. Powers, for instance, created hundreds of portraits but very few ideals, though those were replicated by Powers, sometimes into the hundreds; Hosmer, on the contrary, produced few portraits both relief and in the round, though one of these is a medallion portrait of Gibson, her teacher, and another may have been of Lady Adelaide Talbot, the daughter-in-law of her patron, Marianne Alford. The majority of Hosmer's ideal works, first busts and then full-length figures, are classical themes depicting the nude female, and both *Daphne*, her earliest bust created in Rome in 1853, and her first full-length, a rare depiction of the mourning *Oenone* (Paris's rejected love whom he abandoned when he sought Helen in Troy, again, drawn from Tennyson's poetry), a work of 1854–1855, were sent to her St. Louis patron, Wayman Crow. Crowe had commissioned a full-length figure from Hosmer, who had previously sent *Daphne* as a love-gift; in between she also sculpted a bust of *Medusa* in 1854. Hosmer also authored what are often referred to as "fancy pieces," or "conceits," light-hearted, sometimes humorous genre or imaginative works, such as her most successful (that is, most often replicated) sculpture, *Puck*, of 1855, and its mate, *Will-o'-the-Wisp*, on which she was at work three years later. As with portraiture, this was a sculptural form undertaken fairly often by some of Hosmer's colleagues such as Chauncey B. Ives and Randolph Rogers, and avoided by others such as Powers. Hosmer went on to more challenging sculpture, notably her *Beatrice Cenci* of 1856, based on real-life events of the seventeenth century involving violence and patricide as interpreted in Shelley's 1820 verse drama, *The Cenci*, and the commission in 1857 from the subject's mother to carve the tomb sculpture for *Mlle. Judith (Julie) de Palezieux Falconnet* for the Church of Sant'Andrea della Fratte, the only such monument by any American sculptor in a Roman church.

The concentration on feminine subjects was hardly unusual among the neo-classicists; William Wetmore Story, probably the most celebrated of the American sculptors of Hosmer's generation in Rome, was especially noted for his *Medea*, *Semiramis*, *Sappho*, and countless others, while Randolph Rogers's most famous work—probably the most replicated full-length sculpture of the nineteenth century—was his *Nydia, the Blind Girl of Pompeii*. On the other hand, it should be noted, too, that Hosmer appears, surely deliberately, to have avoided the most common figural subjects so often chosen by her Roman contemporaries, male and female alike. So many images of the biblical Ruth were created that there was talk of "Ruth Fever," among the sculptors at one point, while Cleopatras were created by many colleagues, always contending for variant interpretations. And however much Hosmer's sculptures in general appear to mirror those of her contemporaries, there is often a feminist agenda that they address. *Daphne*, who spurned Apollo, is an allegory of chastity, and Hosmer's *Medusa*, drawn in part from Shelley's "On the Medusa of Leonardo da Vinci," is not the standard image of dread, but a beautiful woman, made horrorific against her will. And *Beatrice Cenci* was viewed as a tragic heroine. It is less surprising then that Hosmer's masterwork, or at least one of her two masterworks, is her sculpture of *Zenobia*. Now a public, rather than private, tragic heroine, Zenobia was one of the great women of history, captured by the Romans and led through the streets in chains, but in Hosmer's sculpture maintaining such monumental dignity, that the work was quite a success when exhibited at the International Exposition in London in 1862, and even thought to have been created by her teacher, John Gibson. It was also well received subsequently when she brought it to New York two years later.

In 1860 Hosmer's St. Louis connections stood her in good stead when she received the commission for the statue of Senator *Thomas Hart Benton* who had died two years before; the monumental figure was to be erected in Lafayette Park. An over-life-size (10 foot) outdoor sculpture and therefore created in bronze at the Royal Foundry in Munich, the most noted foundry of its time, the statue was inaugurated in 1868, almost a decade later, before a hoard of crowds who praised the work, gleaming like gold in the sun. A number of the women sculptors of this group received commissions for full-length portrait images of contemporary and earlier historical figures—Anne Whitney, Vinnie Ream, Emma Stebbins, and Blanche Nevin—commissions often derided by their male contemporaries, artists and laymen, but Hosmer's *Benton* remains one of her most celebrated sculptures. It was also in 1868 that Hosmer created her only other full-length likeness of a contemporary figure and this time still very much alive, depicting the tragic Maria Sophia, the beautiful ex-queen of Naples, who was living in exile in Rome. The sculpture was much praised in its own time, but, unlocated today, it may never have been realized in marble. Having defended her realm against the forces of Garibaldi, Maria Sophia had earned the nickname of the "warrior queen," and thus served as a suitable contemporary counterpart for Hosmer's *Zenobia*. Hosmer's sympathy for the Royalist regimes which were overthrown in the cause of a united Italy surely account for her increasingly lengthy visits to England, though she maintained her studio in Rome. Her final historical sculpture and also her last was the 1892 figure of *Queen Isabella of Spain*, intended for the Columbian Exposition in Chicago in 1893 and afterwards on view in San Francisco in the Mid-Winter Exhibition of 1893–1894, but though exhibited, the work never proceeded beyond the plaster, and may have perished in the earthquake and fire of San Francisco in 1906.

The 1860s witnessed a decline in Hosmer's output, though her work during the decade experienced a number of interesting turns. One of her most successful pieces was *The Sleeping Faun*, which was exhibited to acclaim at the Dublin International Exposition of 1865 and was much replicated. A demure descendant of the famous and very erotic *Barberini Faun* of Antiquity, it nevertheless revealed Hosmer's total competency in the rendering of the male nude. Male ideal figures, clothed or nude, were not nearly as common as were female images, but the male nude was not a rarity in neo-classic sculpture. Perhaps more surprising is the choice of the nude male figure among the women sculptors, though these were few in number. Still, both Emma Stebbins and Anne Whitney created a standing figure of *The Lotus Eater*, again from a poem by Tennyson. Hosmer created a companion sculpture of *The Waking Faun* in 1866, but it is unlocated today and not known to have ever been successfully put into marble. The essence of Hosmer's ideology might be decoded in a comparison of her two sleeping figures—the *Beatrice Cenci* and *The Sleeping Faun*. This goes beyond their obvious difference in gender, and also the distinction between a real, historical figure and a mythological one. The *Cenci* is a heartrending image of a bound young woman, clutching a rosary with a cross, one whose "salvation" lies in her faith in the afterlife. The *Faun* is adorned with an infant satyr, a playful figure which renders the sculpture more in the nature of a large and elaborate, frivolous "conceit." *Beatrice Cenci* will wake and arise only to certain mortal doom; the *Faun* will waken to another day of mischief and playfulness if he awakes at all; perhaps his dormancy is enduring if, in fact, his subsequent complement, *The Waking Faun*, was never realized in marmoreal permanency, but remained in clay or plaster, joining a marble replica of *The Sleeping Faun* in the collection of Lady Ashburton.

Hosmer's friendship with Lady Marianne Alford, begun in the winter of 1860–1861, led the artist into a new phase of her career, which impacted upon her sister sculptors as well. Lady Alford became a major patron of Hosmer's, but in addition to "set" pieces, she also commissioned decorative and monumental works, including the *Fountain of the Sirens*, for her London home at Prince's Gate; Hosmer was working on this from 1861 to 1866. She had previously, in 1858, already been involved in fountain sculpture, working on one that depicted *Hylas and the Water Nymphs*, but the history of this work, presumably also a commission, is not recorded. Such an order from Alford was the beginning not only of a close friendship, but also directed Hosmer more and more toward England as a recipient of her art. It also meant much more security for commissions, provided that the client was pleased, offered financial assurance, especially since these were complicated, often multi-figural works. Hosmer was to spend a good deal of time with Alford, both in London and at Ashford Hall in Hertfordshire. Lady Alford's son, Lord Brownlow, continuing his mother's patronage of the artist, accepted Hosmer's design for gates for the art gallery at Ashford Hall, decorated with sculptural panels, several of which may be identified today as personifications of the stars and the times of day. Lady Ashburton, even far closer to Hosmer than Lady Alford, commissioned several fountains to be placed in the gardens at her country home, Melchet Court in Hampshire, *The Fountain of the Dolphin* and *The Mermaid's Cradle*; several figures from the former still remain with the family, while a much later replica of *The Mermaid's Fountain*, cast in bronze in 1893, adorns Fountain Square in Larchmont, New York. In addition, around 1867 Ashburton commissioned Hosmer for a chimney piece for the drawing room at Melchet Court depicting *The Death of the Dryads*, though this may never have been completed.

Hosmer's involvement in fountain sculpture may have paved the way for further such commissions directed specifically toward her women colleagues. The most notable such work is Emma Stebbins's *Bethesda Fountain*, or *Angel of the Waters*, for New York's Central Park, commissioned in 1863 and installed a decade later. Almost as celebrated was Margaret Foley's most elaborate sculpture, the fountain that was placed in the center of the Horticultural Building at the 1876 Philadelphia Centennial. Anne Whitney created a fountain of children, begun in 1887 and finished four years later, a work exhibited at the Columbian Exposition in Chicago in 1893, while a bronze replica was presented to the city of Boston and another to Newton, Massachusetts, erected in West Newton in 1903. Vinnie Ream designed a fountain of *America* for the state of Missouri, supposedly set in a park in St. Louis, but this has not been located. And later, Blanche Nevin sculptured a *Horse Fountain* for the city of Lancaster, Pennsylvania, where she resided most of her later life.

Overall, Hosmer was America's most famous woman sculptor of the nineteenth century, truly the "leader of the flock." While their number may seem limited compared to the many male sculptors of their era, one might recall that, of the hundreds of women painters active in America during the middle years of the nineteenth century, only one, Lily Martin Spencer, remains a figure of importance in the history of this country's art, and even the recognition and significance of Spencer's paintings, purposefully domestic, is confined to her native land. For the middle years of the nineteenth century, Hosmer's international reputation became, and remains, unique.

Works

HESPER, THE EVENING STAR
2007
watercolor on paper • 15 x 12 in.

Hesper, The Evening Star, 1852
Marble • 24" height
Signed and dated (verso): "Harriet Hosmer"

PROVENANCE

Collection
Present Owners
Watertown Free Public Library, Watertown, MA
Gift of Mrs. Mary Emerson Mead, 1913
Previous Owners
Mary Coolidge, Boston, MA
Dr. Julian Mead, Watertown, MA, 1912
Exhibitions
Cotton's Bookstore, Boston, MA, 1852
Watertown Free Public Library, Watertown, MA, 1923–present

Hesper, The Evening Star is Hosmer's first original sculpture. She modeled and carved it upon her return home to Watertown from the St. Louis Medical College after having successfully obtained her certificate in anatomy. Hosmer sculpted *Hesper* in the backyard studio shed her father built for her behind their home on the Charles River.
Hesperus in Classical Mythology was the son or brother of Atlas. Hesperus was the first to climb Mount Atlas to watch the stars and was swept away by a storm, disappearing without a trace. It is believed he was transformed into the friendly evening star, which brings the peace of night. Hosmer's Hesper was certainly inspired by the British romantic poet Tennyson's 1850 poem, "In Memoriam," which she had memorized.

"Sad Hesper o'er the buried sun
And ready, thou, to die with him,
Thous watchest all things ever dim
And dimmer, and a glory done."

In Hosmer's sculpture, Hesper has a long oval face with droopy eyelids that appear almost closed. Her gaze is lowered. Her shoulders slope downward in a relaxed state and a crescent moon frames her bare chest. The moon's pointy tips contrast the soft heavy weight of Hesper's breasts. Her hair is intricately knotted and twisted with carved stars, shells, and poppies intertwined throughout. These foreshadow the crowns and diadems to come in later works. While some art historians have called this work clumsy, two photographs of this bust and a certificate in anatomy are what convinced John Gibson, the leading neo-classical sculptor living in Rome, to take Hosmer on as his only pupil.
The sleep of night and the eternal sleep of death. Although death was a popular artistic and literary subject in the nineteenth century, and played a central and formative role in Hosmer's life, her subject choice of Hesper seems to be unique.

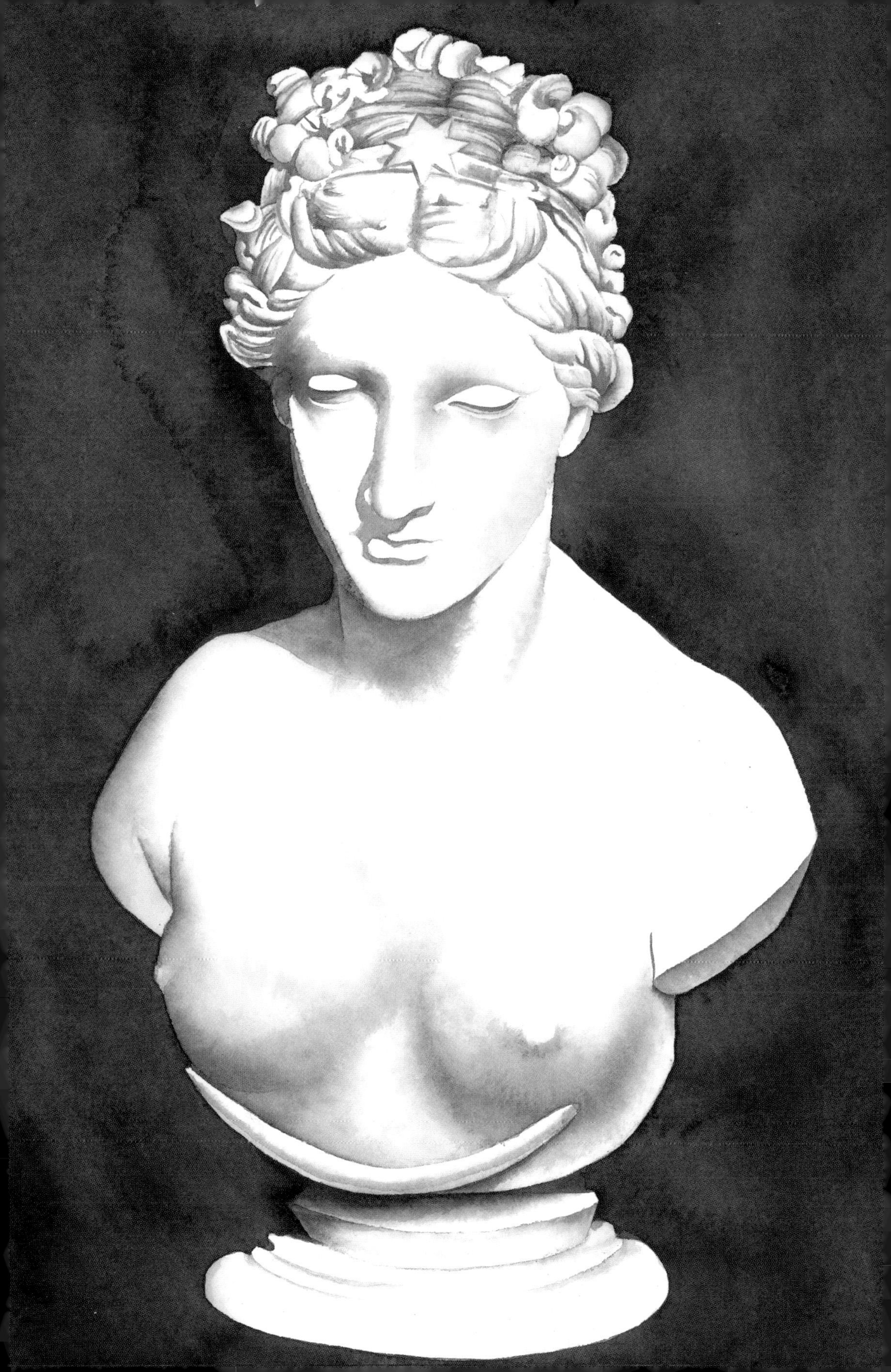

Doctor McDowell

2007
watercolor on paper, 12 x 15 in.

Doctor McDowell, 1852
Marble • Medallion life-size
Signed and dated (verso): unknown

Provenance

Collection
Present Owners
Unknown
Previous Owners
Dr. Joseph McDowell, St. Louis, MO
Exhibitions
St. Louis Medical College, St. Louis, MO, 1859

This is the first portrait of one of many men who had a profound impact on Hosmer's professional life. Knowledge of anatomy was mandatory for a sculptor in the nineteenth century. But women were prohibited from attending college. Hosmer's childhood friend and classmate from Mrs. Sedgwick's school in Lenox, Massachusetts, Cornelia Crow, told her father, Wayman, a wealthy merchant in St. Louis, about Hosmer's predicament. When he heard that Harvard University wouldn't admit Hosmer, he made arrangements for Hosmer to study anatomy with Dr. Joseph Nash McDowell in St. Louis. McDowell was the director of the new St. Louis Medical College and he allowed Hosmer to sit in the back of the room in his anatomy classes.
Once Hosmer successfully completed the coursework with a "diploma of proficiency" she carved this marble medallion and sent it to Dr. McDowell as a token of gratitude. The sculpture's location is unknown today and no photographs of it are known to exist.

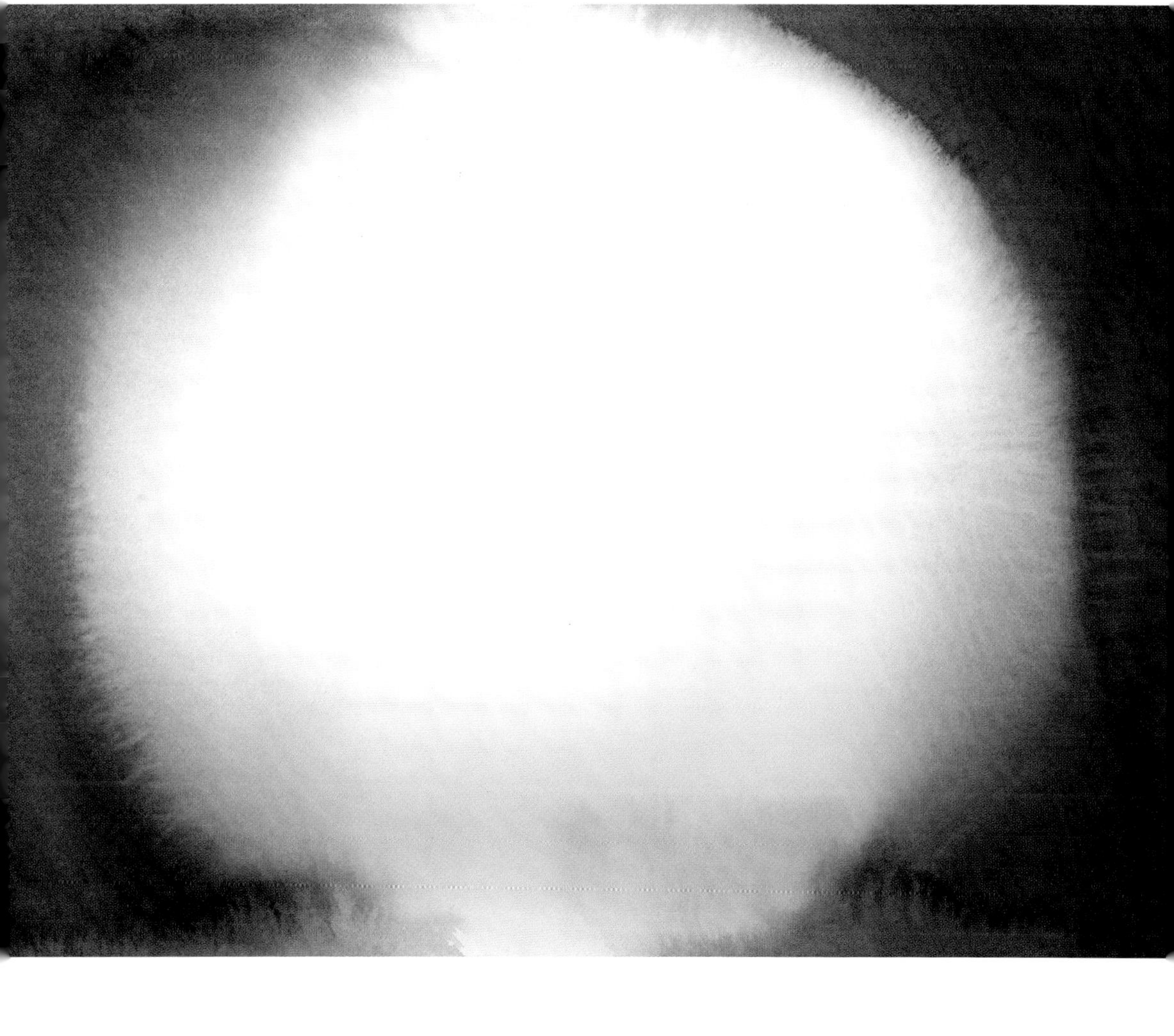

Daphne
2006
watercolor on paper, 15 x 12 in.

Daphne, 1854
Two known versions
Marble • 27.5 x 19 5/8 x 12"
Signed and inscribed (verso): "Harriet Hosmer/ Fecit Romae"

Provenance

Collection
a. *Present Owners*
27 1/2 x 19 5/8 x 12 1/2"
The Metropolitan Museum of Art, New York
Morris K. Jessup Fund, 1973
1973.133
Previous Owners
Clifford O. Devine, New York, NY, 1971
Mrs. Samuel Appleton, Boston, MA
b. *Present Owners*
26 1/2 x 19 1/2 x 13 1/2"
Mildred Lane Kemper Art Museum, St. Louis, MO
Gift of Wayman Crow, Sr., 1880
WU 579
Signed and inscribed (verso into stone pedestal): "HARRIET HOSMER / SCULPT. / ROME"
Previous Owners
Wayman Crow, St. Louis, MO, 1880
Exhibitions
Boston, MA, 1853
Mercantile Library, St. Louis, MO, 1857–1888
Washington University Gallery of Art, St. Louis, MO, 1939, 1940, 1961, 1966
Heritage Show. St. Louis Artists' Guild, Webster Groves, MO, 1963
The White, Marmorean Flock: Nineteenth Century American Neoclassical Sculptors. Vassar College Art Gallery, Poughkeepsie, NY, 1972
200 Years of American Sculpture. Whitney Museum of American Art, New York, NY, 1976
Beginnings: The Taste of the Founders. Washington University Gallery of Art, St. Louis, MO, 2000
Currents of Change: Art and Life Along the Mississippi River, 1850–1861. Minneapolis Institute of Arts, Minneapolis, MN, 2004
Harriet Goodhue Hosmer. Mildred Lane Kemper Museum, St. Louis, MO, 2008
American Wing, Metropolitan Museum of Art, New York, NY, 1986–present

Daphne is Hosmer's first original "ideal" sculpture and the first sculpture Hosmer made in Rome at the beginning of her forty some year career there.
In Classical Mythology and Ovid's *Metamorphoses*, the nymph Daphne vowed perpetual virginity and renounced the love of the god, Apollo. Still, Apollo relentlessly pursued her. At the moment he almost apprehends Daphne, she begs her father, Zeus, to save her and he turns Daphne into a laurel tree.
Hosmer's chaste Daphne is solemn, quiet. She modestly averts her eyes. The bay of laurel not only frame her breasts and shoulders, but contains and restricts her whole being.
Although Daphne was a popular theme for artists it held specific importance for Hosmer, who had denounced marriage:

"You see, everybody is being married but myself. I am the only faithful worshipper of Celibacy, and her service becomes more fascinating the longer I remain in it. Even if so inclined, an artist has no business to marry. For a man, it may be well enough, but for a woman, on whom matrimonial duties and cares weigh more heavily, it is a moral wrong. I think, for she must either neglect her profession or her family, becoming neither a good wife and mother nor a good artist. My ambition is to be the latter, so I wage eternal feud with the consolidating knot."
Letter to Wayman Crow dated August 1854

Although Hosmer never married, she had significant relationships with men, mostly father figures: her own father, Dr. McDowell, Wayman Crow, and John Gibson. The theme of transformation and metamorphosis was a subject she continued to mine throughout her career.

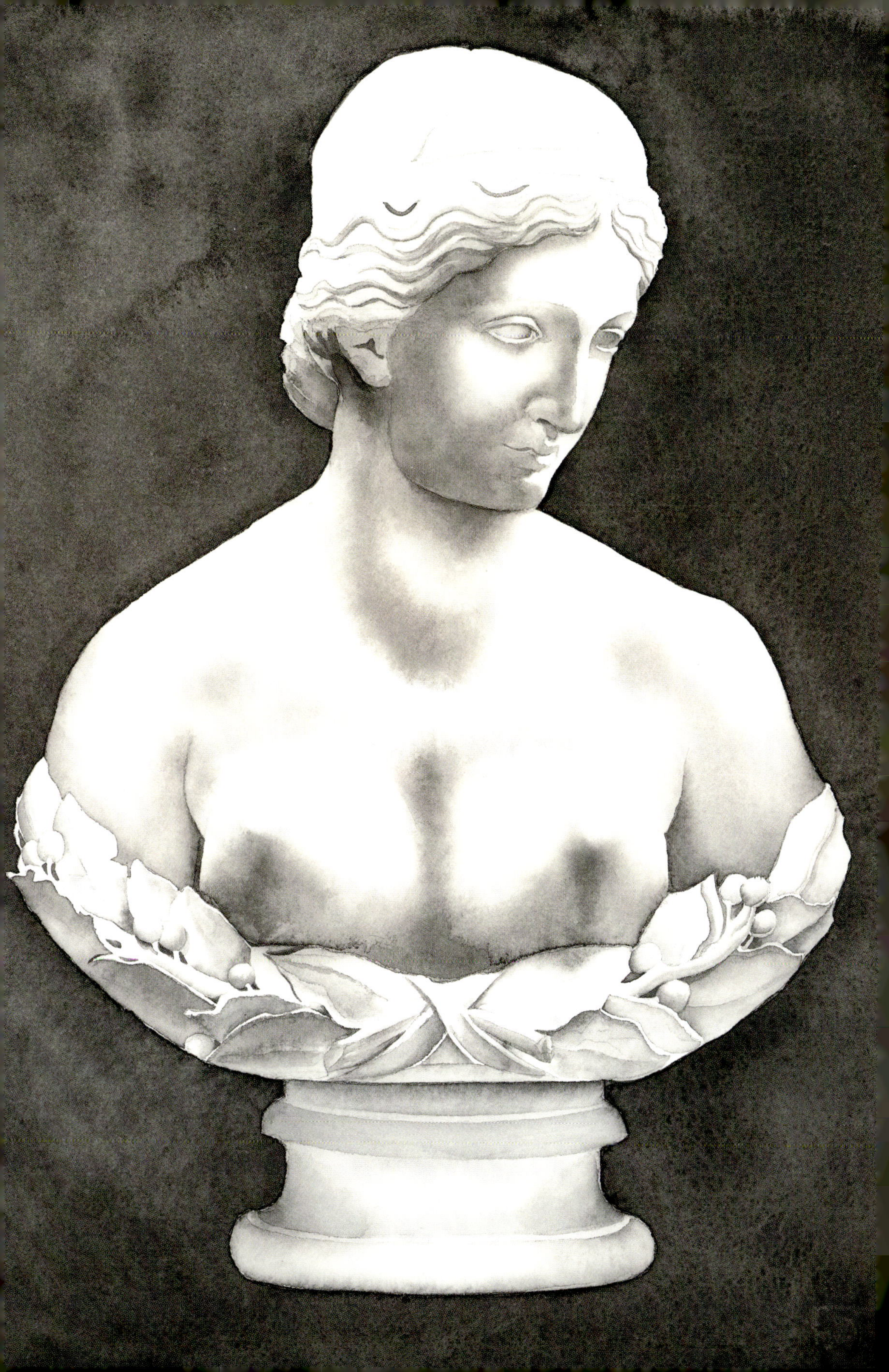

THE CLASPED HANDS OF ROBERT BROWNING AND ELIZABETH BARRETT BROWNING
2006
watercolor on paper, 12 x 15 in.

The Clasped Hands of Robert Browning and Elizabeth Barrett Browning, 1853

Ten known versions (probably more)
Bronze • 3 1/2 x 8 1/4"
Signed, dated, and inscribed (on end of his wrist, etched in the bronze): "HANDS – OF – ROBERT/ AND/Elizabeth Barrett Browning / cast By / Harriet Hosmer / Rome 1853"

PROVENANCE

Collection
a. *Present Owners*
The Metropolitan Museum of Art, New York
Mrs. Frederick A. Stoughton Gift, 1986
1986.52
Previous Owners
Kenny Galleries, 1986
b. *Present Owners*
3 1/2 x 8 x 4"
Armstrong-Browning Library, Baylor University, Waco, TX, 1920
Previous Owners
Harriet Hosmer
Lilian Whiting, Boston, MA
Kate Field
c. *Present Owners*
3 1/4 x 8 x 4 1/2"
Boston Public Library, Rare Book and Manuscript Department, Boston, MA
G. Cab. 3. 79
Previous Owners
Boston Browning Society
d. *Present Owners*
3 1/4 x 8 1/4 x 4 1/2"
Newark Museum, Newark, NJ, 1976
Previous Owners
Mrs. J. G. Phelps Stokes, New York, NY
e. *Present Owners*
3 1/2 x 8 1/2"
Saint Louis Art Museum, St. Louis, MO
Gift of Mrs. Henry Cushman
28:1975
f. *Present Owners*

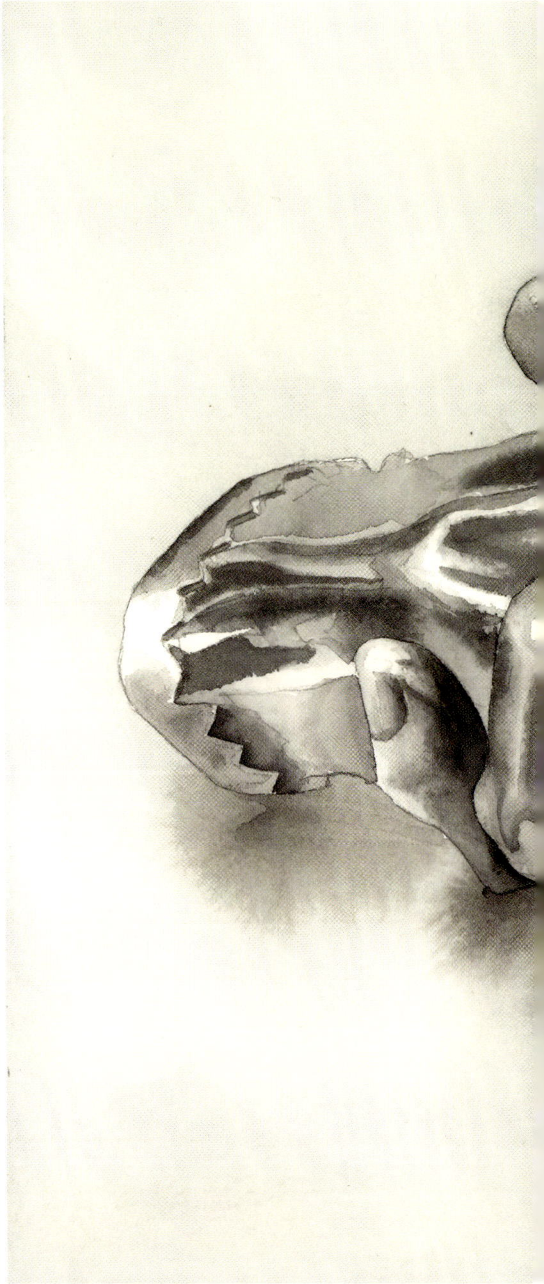

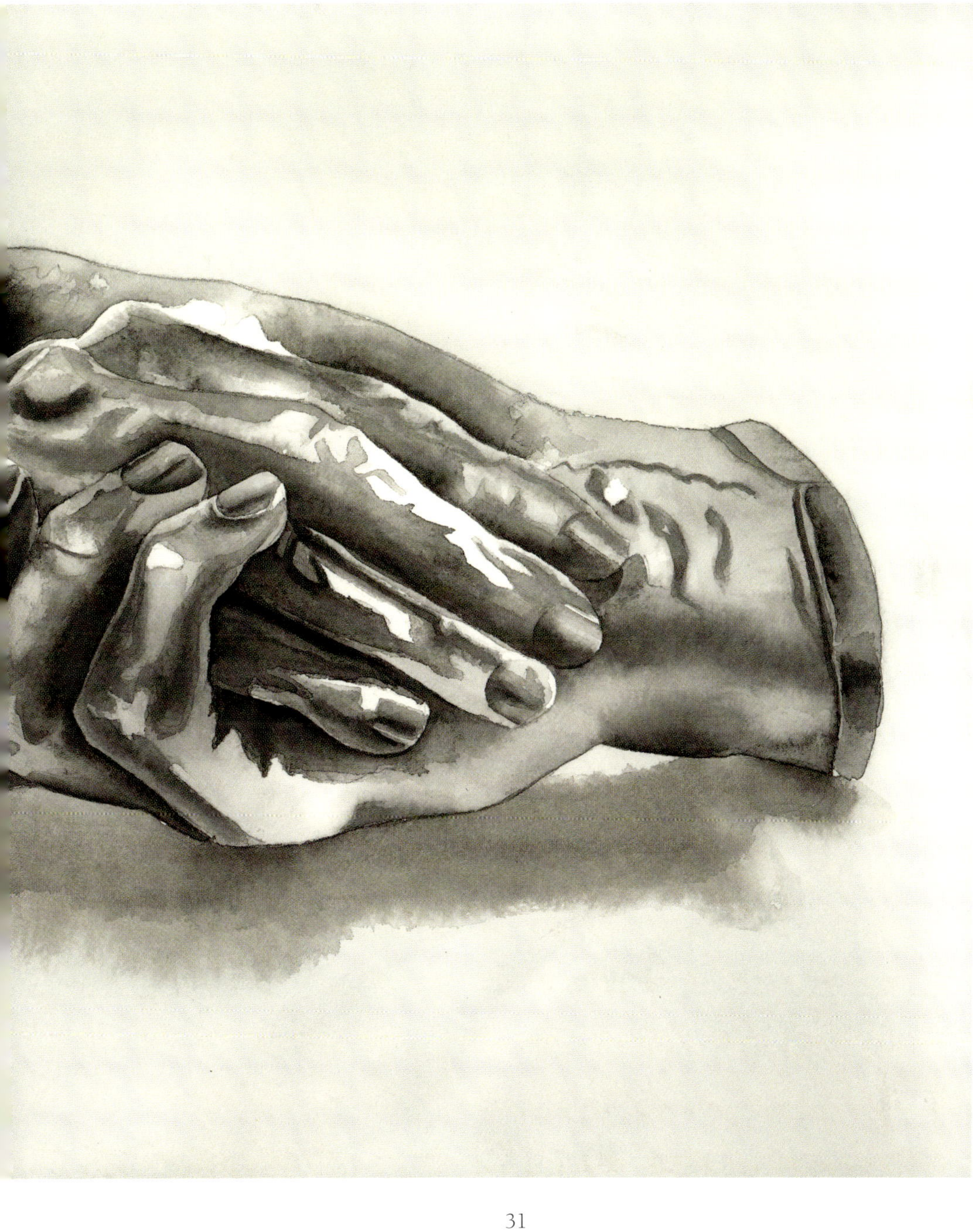

1859
3 1/8 x 8 1/4 x 4 1/4"
Wellesley College
Special Collections
Margaret Clapp Library, Wellesley, MA
Previous Owners
Mrs. Edward Ripley, Chicago, IL, 1895
Mrs. Raphael Pumpelly
Helen Temple Cooke

g. *Present Owners*
Plaster
3 x 8 x 4"
Schlesinger Library, Radcliffe College, Harvard University, Cambridge, MA
Previous Owners
Harriet Hosmer
Mrs. Cornelia Crow Carr, Cambridge, MA
Mrs. Delmar Leighton

h. *Present Owners*
Plaster
National Museum of Women in the Arts, Washington, D.C.

i. *Present Owners*
3 1/2 x 8 1/4"
National Portrait Gallery, London, England
NPG 3165
Previous Owners
William Makepeace Thackeray
Hester Thackeray Fuller (granddaughter of William Makepeace Thackeray)

j. *Present Owners*
3 1/4 x 8 1/4 x 4 1/4"
National Gallery of Art, Washington, D.C.
Gift in Honor of Margaret and Raymond Horowitz
2005.41.1
Previous Owners
Dr. and Mrs. William H. Gerdts, New York, NY

Exhibitions
Centenary of Life and Work of Elizabeth Barrett Browning. St. Marylebone Public Library, London, 1961
Women Artists of America. The Newark Museum, Newark, NJ, 1965
Pine Manor Junior College. Chestnut Hill, MA, 1967
Browning Exhibition. St. Marylebone Public Library, London, 1970
Browning Exhibition. Buckingham Palace Road Library, London, 1970
The White, Marmorean Flock: Nineteenth Century American Neoclassical Sculptors. Vassar College Art Gallery, Poughkeepsie, NY, 1972
American Artists in Europe 1800–1900. Walker Art Gallery, Liverpool, 1976–1977
Aspects of American Sculpture. Hecksher Museum, Huntington, NY, 1983
American Bronze Sculpture: 1850 to the Present. The Newark Museum, Newark, NJ, 1985
American Women Artists, 1830–1930. National Museum of Women in the Arts, Washington, D.C., 1987
Musée d'Orsay, Paris, 2002
Second Skin: Contemporary and Historical Live Casting. Henry Moore Institute, Leeds, 2002
Hamburger Kunsthalle, Hamburg, 2002
Museo Vela, Ligornetto, 2002
Harriet Goodhue Hosmer. Mildred Lane Kemper Museum, St. Louis, MO, 2008
Picturing America. The Newark Museum, Newark, NJ, 2001–present
Metropolitan Museum of Art, New York, NY, 1986–present

Although nineteenth-century sculptors frequently took orders for and produced multiple original marble sculptures from the same design, it wasn't until the mid-1850s that artists started casting multiple replicas in bronze. This sculpture is Hosmer's first bronze. It is the only sculpture Hosmer created that is a human fragment and the only finished work of art she cast directly from her subject. The subjects are her famous friends: the poets Elizabeth Barrett Browning and Robert Browning. There are plaster and bronze versions. Hosmer made a mould of their joined hands from life, insuring the specificity of the poets' physiognomy. This is the antithesis of the neoclassical ideal. "Bonded bronze" copies, otherwise

known as plaster knock offs, can still be purchased in the Metropolitan Museum gift shop.
The Brownings were the most famous members of the Anglo-American expatriate community of writers and artists that lived in Florence and Rome in the nineteenth century. Hosmer met them during her second winter in Rome and they became fast friends. As major literary figures of their time—this friendship was celebrated in their writing and letters. Mrs. Browning wrote about Hosmer's *Medusa* in her novel, *Aurora Leigh,* and their correspondence was lively.
The sculpture consists of Robert and Elizabeth's right hands, one hand clasping the other in the symbol of marriage. Her small, frail hand with the slightly swollen knuckles of a person older than her forty-seven years is framed with a scalloped cuff of a blouse. Robert's hand is only slightly more imposing. His fingers are larger and longer while his thumb holds her hand firmly. They are not the passive loose grip of young love, but a pact, active, and purposefully posed. Because the piece is relatively small, lightweight, and three dimensionally complete in the round, the owner can decide and place almost any side down toward the base choosing which of the hands is more dominant to the viewer. The hands do not have the polished honed finish of Hosmer's marble surfaces. They are exactly how they came out of the mold.
The work seems to do two things: celebrate heterosexual love and publicize the friendship of the poets and the artist.

Medusa
2006
watercolor on paper, 15 x 12 in.

Medusa, 1854
Three known versions
Marble • 27 1/4 x 18 1/2 x 9"
Signed and inscribed (verso): "HARRIET HOSMER/SCULPt/ROME"

Provenance

Collection
a. *Present Owners*
Detroit Institute of Arts, Detroit, MI
Founders Society Purchase
Robert H. Tannahill Foundation Fund, 1976
76.6
Previous Owners
Possibly Mrs. Samuel Appleton, Boston, MA, 1855–?
Possibly Mr. & Mrs. John Bullard, Brooklyn, NY, 1872
George William Curtis, Ashfield, MA, ?–1892
William C. Curtis, Ashfield, MA, 1892–1941
Ashfield auction house, 1942
New York Collector, 1942–1961
John B. Friend, Shelburne Falls, NY, 1961–1971
Graham Williford, NY, 1971–1975
Shepherd Gallery, NY, 1975
b. *Present Owners*
27 1/4 x 21 x 9 1/2"
Minneapolis Institute of the Arts, Minneapolis, MN
The Walter C. and Mary C. Briggs Purchase Fund
2003.125
Signed and inscribed (verso): "HARRIETHOSMER/ROME"
Previous Owners
Blue Hill Corporation, Kent, England, 1925–2000
Mr. D. Hall, Kent, England, 2000–2002
Acquired from Conner/Rosenkranz American Sculpture, New York, NY
c. *Present Owners*
27 1/2 x 19 x 9 1/2"
Hood Art Museum, Dartmouth College, Dartmouth, NH
Purchased through a Gift from Jane and W. David Dance, Class of 1940
S.996.24
May 22, 1996 (Sotheby's, Sale 6854, lot 108)
Signed and inscribed (verso): "HARRIET HOSMER / SCULPt ["t" is above horizontal line and two periods] / ROME"
Previous Owners
A.L. Burgress, Mt. Holly, NJ, 1968
Mr. and Mrs. Bullard, Brooklyn, NY, 1872
Mr. and Mrs. Drew Peters, Sarasota, FL, 1980

Exhibitions
Boston, MA, 1853
London International Exhibition, London, 1862
The White Marmorean Flock: Nineteenth Century American Women Neoclassical Sculptors. Vassar College Art Gallery, 1972
December Treasure of the Month. Museum of Fine Arts, Saint Petersburg, FL, 1992
Hood Museum of Art, Dartmouth College, Hanover, NH, 1997, 2004, 2005–2007
National Gallery of Ireland, Dublin, Ireland, 2002
Van Gogh Museum, Amsterdam, The Netherlands, 2002–2003
Musée d'Art Americain, Giverny, France, 2003
Phoenix Art Museum, Phoenix, AZ, 2003–2004
Currents of Change: Art and Life Along the Mississippi River 1850–1861. Minneapolis Institute of Arts, Minneapolis, MN, 2004
San Diego Museum of Art, San Diego, CA, 2004
American Beauty: Paintings and Sculptures From The Detroit Institute of Arts. The Detroit Institute of Arts, Detroit, MI, 2002–2005
Milwaukee Art Museum, Milwaukee, WI, 2004–2005
Frick Art & Historical Center, Pittsburgh, PA, 2005

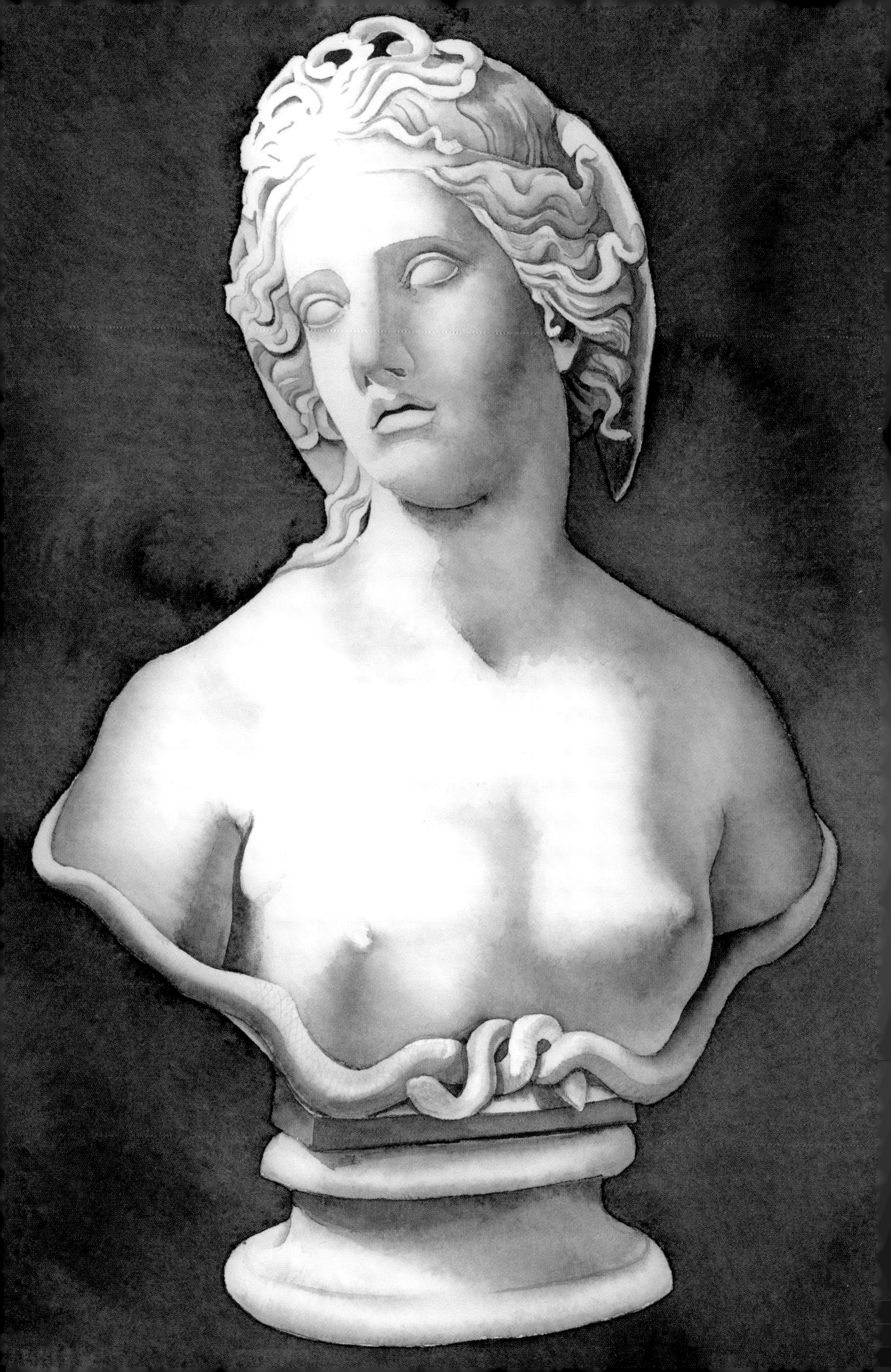

Critical Faculties: Teaching with the Hood's Collections. Hood Museum of Art, Dartmouth College, Hanover, NH, 2005
American Art at Dartmouth: Highlights from the Hood Museum of Art. Hood Museum of Art, Dartmouth College, Hanover, NH, 2007

Medusa is Hosmer's first commissioned sculpture, her third consecutive female bust; her second bust with the theme of metamorphosis and the companion to her *Daphne* (1853). All have exposed breasts.

In Greek Mythology, Medusa was the only mortal and the most beautiful of the three Gorgon sisters. After angering Athena by having an affair with Poseidon, Athena retaliated and transformed Medusa into a repulsive being with snakes for hair along with a powerful gaze that literally petrified men, turning them to stone. Perseus decapitated Medusa to protect his mother, Danae, from King Polydectes. Once beheaded, two beings were born from her neck: Chrysaor and Pegasus.

Hosmer's depiction of *Medusa* with its neo-classical restraint and attractive face is in stark contrast to Bernini's baroque caricature (1644–1648), complete with a swarm of writhing snakes on her head, still on view at the Musei Capitolini in Rome. Hosmer challenges this dominant, and perhaps male, visual and literary tradition by invoking the alternate story of Medusa. Hosmer was undoubtedly aware of the serene *Rondanini Medusa*, a Roman copy of a classical work from the fifth century BCE which provided an alternative interpretation of the myth, more in line with Hosmer's.

Hosmer portrays Medusa not simply as beautiful but sympathetic as well. Her head is tilted back and up. She is looking away, not directly at the viewer. We are watching her gaze and yet, while she is performing this, her most powerful activity, her chest and breasts are left vulnerable and exposed. Her shoulders are relaxed, her truncated arms end discreetly at her deltoids. They are slightly pushed back, placing her chest forward facing the viewer, unguarded with a decorative knot of two snakes joining delicately under her breasts. Behind her undulating locks of hair are hidden two wings that reference her most famous offspring, Pegasus. By depicting Medusa in her pre-decapitated state, her head firmly attached to her body, Hosmer stresses her humanity. The wings allude to her fate, the final chapter in her metamorphosis.

Puck
2007
watercolor on paper, 15 x 12 in.

Puck, 1855
Twelve known versions (probably at least thirty)
Marble • 30 7/8 x 15 1/2 x 19 3/4"
Signed and inscribed (verso): "HARRIET HOSMER FECIT – ROMAE"

Provenance

Collection
a. *Present Owners*
1856
Chrysler Museum of Art, Norfolk, VA
Gift of James H. Ricau and Museum Purchase, 1986
86.471
Previous Owners
James H. Ricau, Piermont, NY, 1964
Louis Joseph, Boston, MA
b. *Present Owners*
30 1/2 x 16 5/8 x 19 5/8"
1856
Smithsonian American Art Museum, Washington, D.C.
Gift of Mrs. George Merrill
Signed, and inscribed and dated (on base, recto): "HARRIET HOSMER, Sculp. 1856"
1918.3.5
Previous Owners
Mrs. Smith-Cliff, NY
Mrs. George Merrill Washington, D.C.
c. *Present Owners*
Watertown Free Public Library, Watertown, MA
Gift of Rev. Joseph L. Curran, in memory of Katherine M. Bell, 1992
Previous Owners
Rev. Joseph L. Curran, Watertown, MA
d. *Present Owners*
Lenox Library Association, Lenox, MA
Gift of Harriet C. Weed, Newburgh, NY, 1952
Previous Owners
Edward Hubert Litchfield, MI
Parke Bernet Galleries New York, NY, 1951
e. *Present Owners*
34 x 14 x 20"
Art Gallery of New South Wales, Sydney, Australia
Bequest of Judge Josephson, 1892
1167
Signed and inscribed (on base, verso): "HARRIET HOSMER/ROMA"
1918.3.5
Previous Owners
Judge Joshua Frey Josephson, 1892
f. *Present Owners*
Senate Chambers of Barbados, Bridgetown, Barbados
Inscribed: "Presented to the colony of Barbados by Lady Briggs in Memory of her husband Sir Thomas Graham Briggs, Bart."
Previous Owners
Lady Briggs, 1918
g. *Present Owners*
Walker Art Center, Liverpool, England
h. *Present Owners*
National Portrait Gallery, London, England
1976
WAG 9117
Previous Owners
Prince of Wales
i. *Present Owners*
Borough Museum, Kendal, England
Signed and inscribed: "H Hosmer Fecit Romae"
Gift of Mr. Jacob Wakefield, Sedgwick House, 1948
j. *Present Owners*
31 x 14 x 17 1/2"
Signed and inscribed (base verso): "H Hosmer/Rome"
The Huntington Library, Art Collections, and Botanical Gardens, San Marino, CA
Purchased with funds from the Virginia Steele Scott Foundation
91.255
Previous Owners
R.A. Carter, Los Angeles, CA
JoAnn & Julian Ganz Jr., Los Angeles, CA, 1979–1989
k. *Present Owners*
1856
31 x 13 1/2 x 20"
Signed and inscribed (verso): "HARRIET HOSMER FECIT. ROMAE."
(on integral base, recto): "PUCK."
Forest Hills Cemetery and the Forest Hills

Educational Trust, Boston, MA
Previous Owners
Purchased at Skinner's auction 1990

l. *Present Owners*
1856
31 x 13 1/2 x 20"
Signed and inscribed (verso): "HARRIET HOSMER FECIT. ROMAE."
(on integral base, recto): "PUCK."
Dr. and Mrs. William H. Gerdts, New York, NY
Previous Owners
Purchased from Post Road Gallery, Larchmont, NY, 2003

Exhibitions
Boston Athenaeum, Boston, MA, 1857
London International Exhibition, London, 1862
National Academy of Design, New York, NY, 1865
19th-Century America: Paintings and Sculptures. The Metropolitan Museum of Art, New York, NY, 1970
An American Perspective: 19th-Century Art from the Collection of Jo Ann and Julian Ganz, Jr. National Gallery of Art, Washington, D.C. (traveled to Amon Carter Museum, Fort Worth, TX and Los Angeles County Museum of Art, Los Angeles, CA), 1982
Images of Innocence: The Child in American Art. Smithsonian American Art Museum, Washington, D.C., 1987–1990
The Ricau Collection. The Chrysler Museum, Norfolk, VA, 1989
Rave Reviews: One Hundred Years of Great American Art. National Academy of Design, New York, NY (traveled to Gilcrease Museum, Tulsa, OK), 2000–2001
Young America: Treasures from the Smithsonian American Art Museum. Smithsonian American Art Museum, Washington, D.C., 2000–2003

Puck is Hosmer's first "fancy piece" or "conceit," as such work was known in the nineteenth century. It was a terrific financial success at the time, selling for \$500–\$1,000. Hosmer said it was worth its weight in silver. She is reported to have made thirty of them. But, she probably rounded down, insuring their value.
Based on Shakespeare's *A Midsummer Night's Dream*, Puck, also known as Robin Goodfellow is:

"that shrewd and knavish sprite
Call'd Robin Goodfellow: are not you he
That frights the maidens of the villagery;
Skim milk, and sometimes labour in the quern
And bootless make the breathless housewife churn;
And sometime make the drink to bear no barm;
Mislead night-wanderers, laughing at their harm?
Those that Hobgoblin call you and sweet Puck,
You do their work, and they shall have good luck:
Are not you he?"

An art historical reference in Hosmer's piece include Roman copies of Greek Hellenistic sculptures of children, especially Spinario's *Boy with a Goose* that is in the Vatican Museum collection. The idea to neutralize a potentially dangerous subject by depicting Puck as more of a child than a sexualized adolescent, may have originated with Sir Joshua Reynold's painting *Puck* for the Boydell Shakespeare Gallery. In it, Puck is a literal babe in the woods, depicted seated on a mushroom with arms playfully raised.
Hosmer's Puck sits on a toadstool. He is a prankster, a woodland sprite with abundant folds of baby flesh crying out to be squeezed. He is seated on his mushroom throne getting ready to pitch a beetle at the viewer with his right hand and tries to hold a lizard, its tail climbing up his forearm, in his left. He wears a seashell for a hat, his curling locks of hair wave. Two nearly translucent bat wings attach to his back. Puck's chubby legs are crossed, eclipsing/obscuring a clear view of his decidedly infant-sized penis. The crossed legs for modesty were in keeping with the decorum of Hosmer's era. His big toe on his right foot points up, almost asking to be pulled. The variety of textures of the foliage growing underneath him is impressive and varied. Clusters of smaller mushrooms, acanthus leaves, and flowers change slightly in arrangement from sculpture to sculpture, but Puck himself remains constant.
Perhaps Hosmer sculpted a baby boy (albeit of the fairy tale or myth) so she might be viewed as accepting her proper role—that of mother. This would counter-balance her more powerful, even proto-feminist, depictions of independent women. She even referred to Oenone and Puck as mother and son.

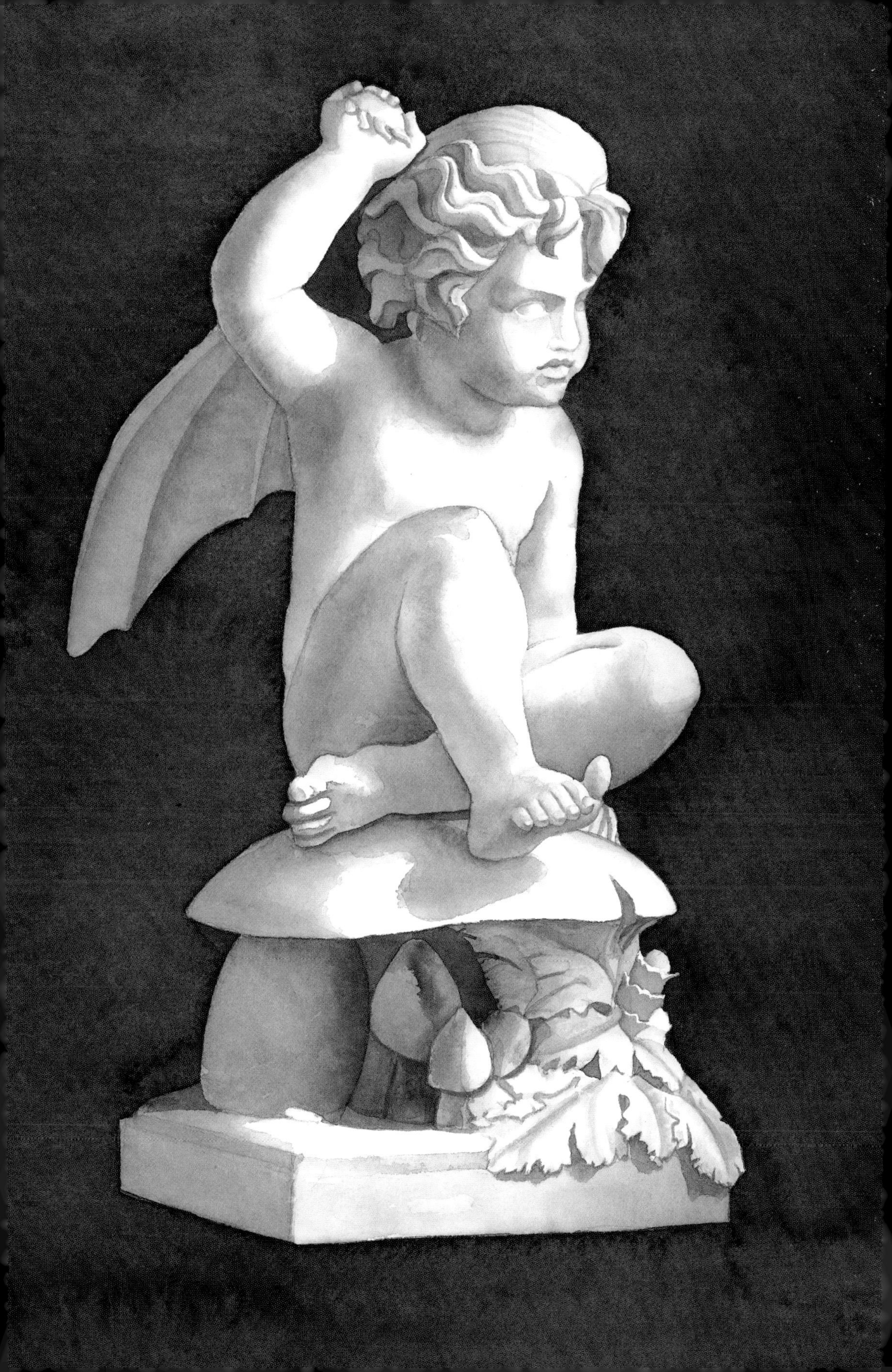

Oenone
2006
watercolor on paper, 12 x 15 in.

Oenone, 1854–1855
Marble • 33 3/8 x 34 3/4 x 26 3/4"
Signed and inscribed (on base, recto): "OENONE (on base, verso): HARRIET HOSMER / FECIT ROME"

Provenance

Collection
Present Owners
Mildred Lane Kemper Art Museum, St. Louis, MO
Gift of Wayman Crow, Sr., 1885
WU 3783
Previous Owners
Wayman Crow Sr., St. Louis, MO, 1885
Exhibitions
Four Centuries of American Art. Minneapolis Institute of Arts, Minneapolis, MN, 1964
The White, Marmorean Flock: Nineteenth Century American Neoclassical Sculptors. Vassar College Art Gallery, Poughkeepsie, NY, 1972
Nature and the Figure. Washington University Gallery of Art, St. Louis, MO, 1983
Nineteenth-Century Art from the Collection. Washington University Gallery of Art, St. Louis, MO, 1986
Beginnings: The Taste of the Founders. Washington University Gallery of Art, St. Louis, MO, 2000
Collecting Patterns. Washington University Gallery of Art, St. Louis, MO, 2003
Harriet Goodhue Hosmer. Mildred Lane Kemper Museum, St. Louis, MO, 2008

Oenone is Hosmer's first full-size figure. It was commissioned by Wayman Crow.

In Greek Mythology, Oenone was a shepherdess (nymph) from Mount Ida and the bride of Paris. When Paris abandoned Oenone for Helen of Troy, Oenone told him that if he were wounded he would have to return to her because she was the only one who could heal him. In exchange for her virginity, Apollo had given her the knowledge of medicine. Paris was wounded and returned to Oenone, who in anger refused to heal him. Repentant, she changed her mind too late. When she heard that Paris had died, she was so overcome with grief and remorse that she committed suicide.

The visual precedent for Hosmer's Oenone subject could have been the Roman copy of the Greek Hellenistic statue *Nymph with Shell* that was in Palazzo Borghese and now in the Louvre Museum. The seated nymph pose is similar to Hosmer's. The literary inspiration would have been Tennyson's poem "Oenone," which was well known at the time. Hosmer focuses on an earlier moment in the story, the abandonment of Oenone. Betrayed and rejected, Oenone is classically seated and half naked. She gazes down at her unused shepherd's staff. Her body is heavy with sadness; one arm braces and supports her upper torso. Her rivulets of hair are pulled back in a bun. Her head is reminiscent of Hosmer's idealized head of Daphne. One foot and one hand extend past the base of the statue.

Hosmer's displeasure over her close friend, Cornelia Crow's marrying to Lucien Carr, probably fueled the inspiration for this work. Hosmer felt betrayed and abandoned herself, and communicated these feelings in letters to Cornelia. It is unlikely that it was a coincidence that she decided to make this particular sculpture when Cornelia's father, Wayman Crow, commissioned a full figure from her. Since Hosmer designed this piece destined for the Crow home, it is clear that she was injecting her specific content into her aesthetic choices.

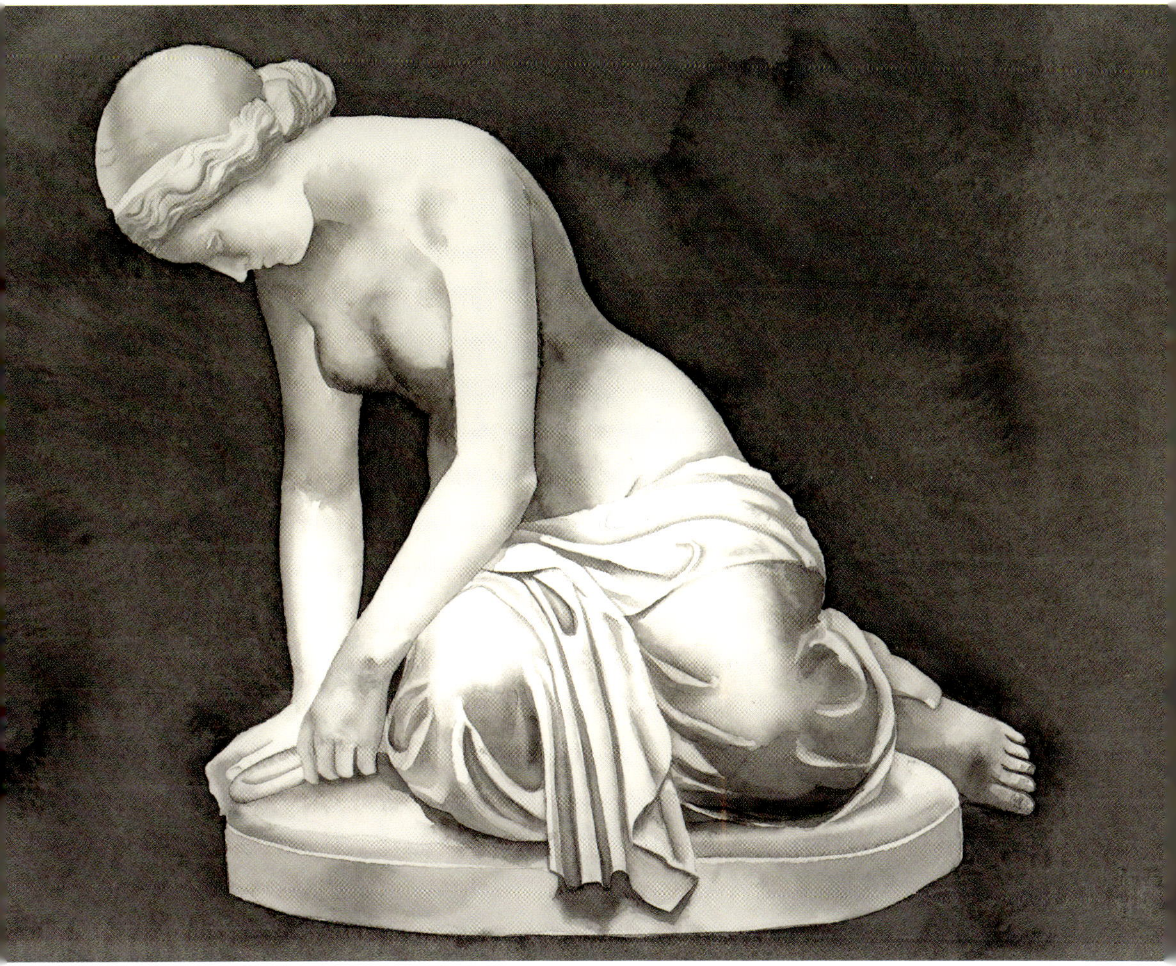

Beatrice Cenci
2007
watercolor on paper, 12 x 15 in.

Beatrice Cenci, 1856
Marble • 24 x 64 x 23 1/2"
Signed and inscribed (verso, lower center, carved in marble): "Harriet Hosmer sculpsit Romae"

Provenance

Collection
a. *Present Owners*
St. Louis Mercantile Library, University Missouri, St. Louis, MO
M266.1856.001
Previous Owners
Commissioned for the St. Louis Mercantile Library
b. *Present Owners*
17 3/8 x 42 8/7 x 17 1/4"
Signed (on base, verso): "HARRIET HOSMER ROMA"
Art Gallery of New South Wales, Sydney, Australia
Previous Owners
Judge Joshua Frey Josephson, 1892
Exhibitions
Royal Academy of Arts, London, 1857
English Art Exhibition, NY Academy of Design, New York, NY, 1857
St. Louis Mercantile Library, St. Louis, MO, 1857–present

Beatrice Cenci is Hosmer's first full-size work of a historic figure.
Beatrice Cenci (?–1599) was, by all accounts including legal, sexually abused by her notorious father, Count Francesco Cenci, who also treated her siblings and his wife intolerably. Count Cenci was already sentenced to death three times for sodomy. But he bribed Pope Clement VIII (1592–1605) and remained free. Beatrice conspired with her brothers and stepmother to end their abusive relationship with the Count by hiring two men to kill him. They drugged Count Cenci and led him out onto a sabotaged balcony, where he plunged to his death. Beatrice, her stepmother, and brothers were put on trial. Many citizens and prominent Italians unsuccessfully petitioned for their release. The Pope sided with the Count, perhaps because he wanted the large Cenci estate. The entire family was sentenced to death. Giacomo was drawn and quartered. Beatrice and her stepmother were beheaded. The youngest brother's life was spared, but the Church took the Cenci estate.
The scandalous story struck a chord with the eighteenth- and nineteenth-century artists and writers, most famously Percy Bysshe Shelley's "The Cenci" (1819), with which Hosmer certainly would have been familiar:

"No, Mother, we must die:
Since such is the reward of innocent lives;
Such the alleviation of worst wrongs.
And whilst our murderers live, and hard, cold men,
Smiling and slow, walk thro' a world of tears
To death as to life's sleep; 'twere just the grave
Were some strange joy for us. Come, obscure Death,
And wind me in thine all-embracing arms!
Like a fond mother hide me in thy bosom,
And rock me to the sleep from which none wake."

An aesthetic influence for Hosmer's Cenci was Guido Reni's famous portrait of Cenci, painted from life while Cenci was awaiting execution in her Castel Sant'Angelo cell. The painting hung in the Palazzo Barberini which Hosmer frequented. Many copies of this very popular painting were widely circulated and collected.
Hosmer's Cenci is a beautiful young woman laying down in a childlike pose with the diaphanous folds of drapery sensually clinging to her adolescent body, her curling locks of hair cascading down her back. Hosmer blends a girl/woman ideal and emphasizes her vulnerability. Her limp hand can barely hold her rosary. Her eyes are closed and she appears peacefully asleep. Cenci is portrayed in her dungeon, as evidenced by the ringbolt attached to her prison block, which supports her torso. The execution is imminent and she is at peace.
The dominant theme of a power struggle between a daughter and a father in which the daughter resists being controlled, resonated strongly with Hosmer. Her own father had just stopped his financial support. It is interesting then that Hosmer chose to heroicize a young woman convicted of patricide. The immense popularity of the story would also guarantee the sculpture's success.

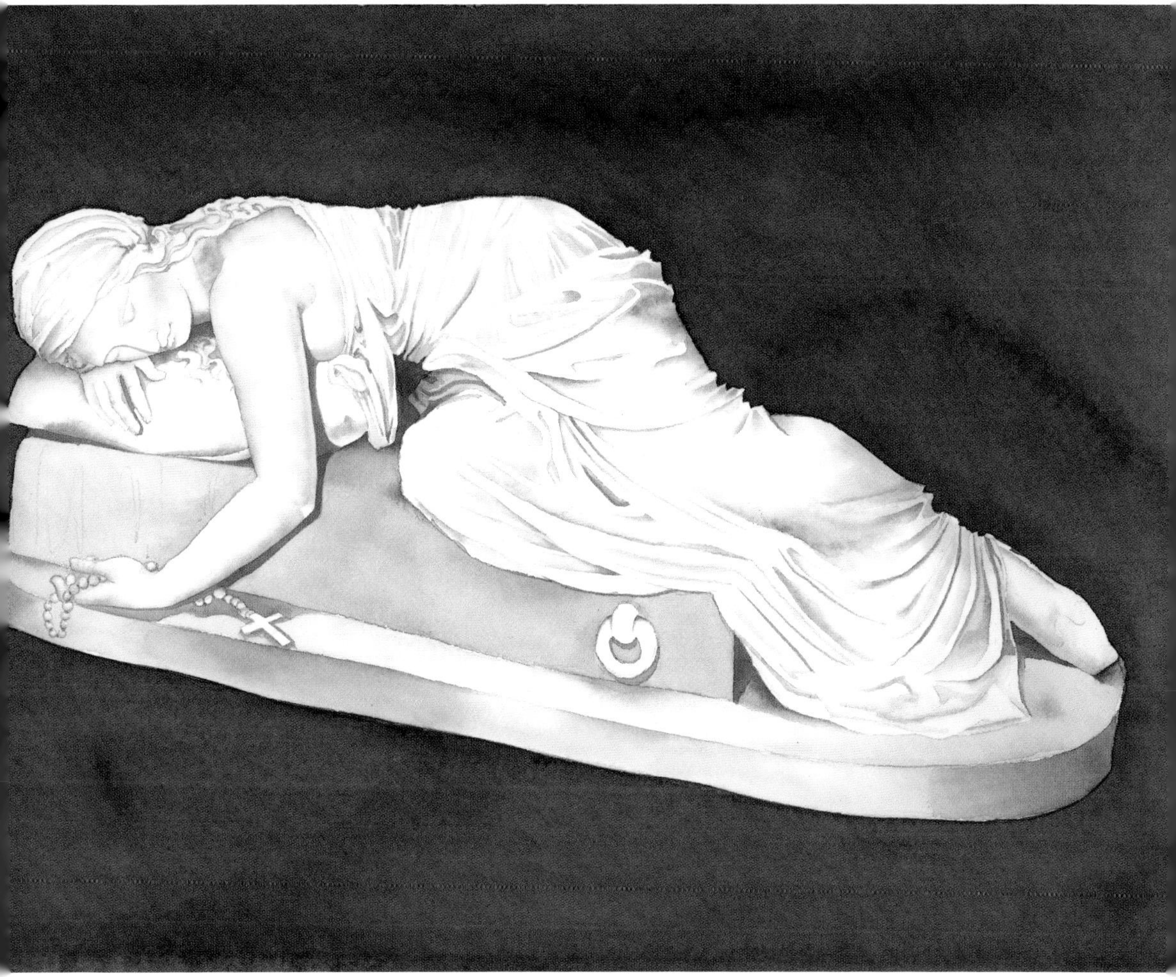

Lady Constance Talbot
2007
watercolor on paper, 12 x 15 in.

Lady Constance Talbot, 1857
Marble bas-relief • Medallion 15" circa diameter
Signed and dated (verso): unknown

Provenance

Collection
Present Owners
Watertown Free Public Library, Watertown, MA
Gift of Harriet Hosmer Carr, 1923
Previous Owners
Harriet Hosmer Carr
Exhibitions
Watertown Free Public Library, Watertown, MA, 1923–present

This is the only known Hosmer medallion that is a bas relief portrait of a woman.

Lady Constance Talbot was a British aristocratic friend of Hosmer's. She was the granddaughter of Lady Marion Alford, who was one of Hosmer's lovers and also one of her biggest collectors.

The medallion is delicately carved. Talbot's face is calm, she looks to the right. Her long hair is neatly curled into a bun that is held in a decorative hairnet. It is impressive how much depth and volume Hosmer conveys in a piece of marble that is only one inch thick.

While most artists continually created lucrative portrait busts and medallions throughout their career, Hosmer seems to only have made them for people she deeply cared for: Dr. McDowell, John Gibson, Wayman Crow, and this one of Lady Constance Talbot.

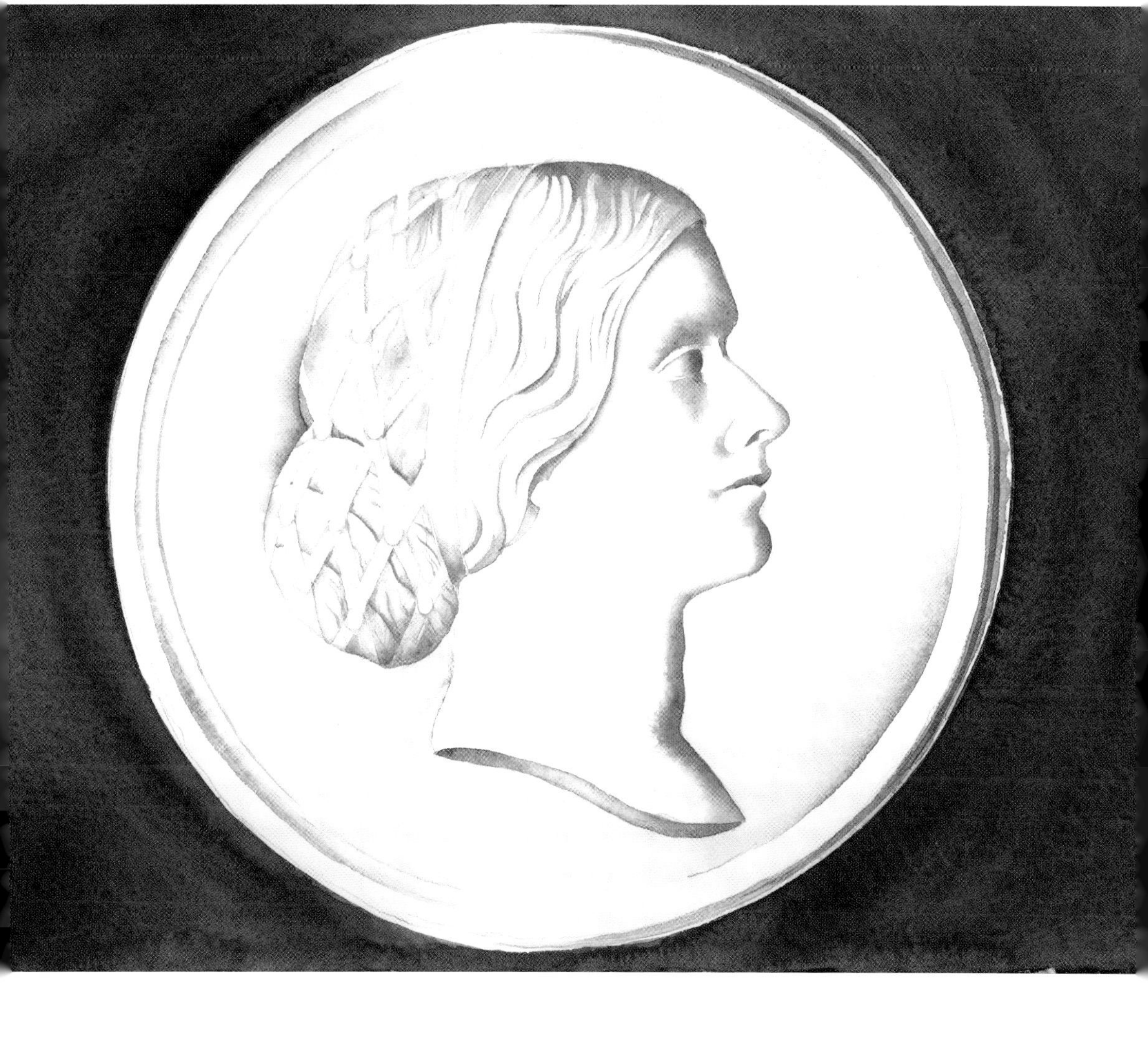

Tomb of Judith Falconnet
2006
watercolor on paper, 12 x 15 in.

Tomb of Judith Falconnet, 1857–1858
Marble • Life-size

Provenance

Collection
Present Owners
Church of Sant'Andrea della Fratte, Rome
Signed and dated (verso): "Harriet Hosmer Fecit Romae"
Inscribed on marble shelf (verso): "IN MEMORIAM JUDITH DE PALEZIEUX FALCONNET MDCCCLVL"
Exhibitions
Church of Sant'Andrea della Fratte, Rome, 1857–present

The *Tomb of Judith Falconnet* is the first artwork by an American artist, male or female, permanently installed in a Roman Church, Sant'Andrea della Fratte, and the only example of funerary art in Hosmer's oeuvre. Because Hosmer was raised Protestant, it was unusual for a non-Catholic to receive a commission for a Catholic tomb. It was even more unusual that a woman was commissioned at the time. Commissions for churches were not only the most prestigious, publicly and eternally on view, but also the most lucrative.

Ms. Falconnet's identity, cause of death, and the explanation for the location of the tomb in the church are unknown. The church served a largely non-Italian congregation. Ms. Falconnet's mother was English and historians have speculated that John Gibson may have played a role in securing the commission for Hosmer.

The tomb is one of thirty-five monuments to the dead in the seventeenth-century church designed by Boromini. Hosmer's statue is located in the St. Francis de Sales Chapel, the third chapel on the right. The chapel has a central polychrome altar, an eighteenth-century altarpiece, and a seated life-size marble effigy of Cardinal Pier Luigi Carafa on the left wall with two winged skulls in the corners. On the right wall above eye level is Hosmer's white marble tomb sculpture of sixteen-year-old Judith de Palezieux Falconnet. An arched background panel of darker marble contrasts with the virginal figure that lies on a Roman day bed, as if taking a nap. Her simple nightgown has horizontal geometric folds; one hand holds a rosary, and the other rests by her side. Her legs are chastely crossed. Her eyes, which are barely formed, blur the boundary between sleep and death. It is rare to depict a solitary female figure, especially an adolescent, without parents or spiritual attendants that might assist in the transport from earthly to spiritual life. Hosmer's spiritualism and neo-classical tenants of restraint reject baroque depictions of religious ecstasy. In their place is a minimalist transition from this life to the next. The dignified simplicity of the tomb is devoid of the ornamentation of renaissance tombs and contrasts with the baroque expressionism of the St. Francis de Sales Chapel and the entire church.

Death was not an abstraction for Hosmer. Her mother and three siblings had died of consumption by the time she was twelve years old. Her sister Helen died at fourteen, when Hosmer was twelve. A little more than a decade later Hosmer was sculpting the dead body of a sixteen-year-old girl. This undoubtedly contributed to the solemnity and dignity of her design.

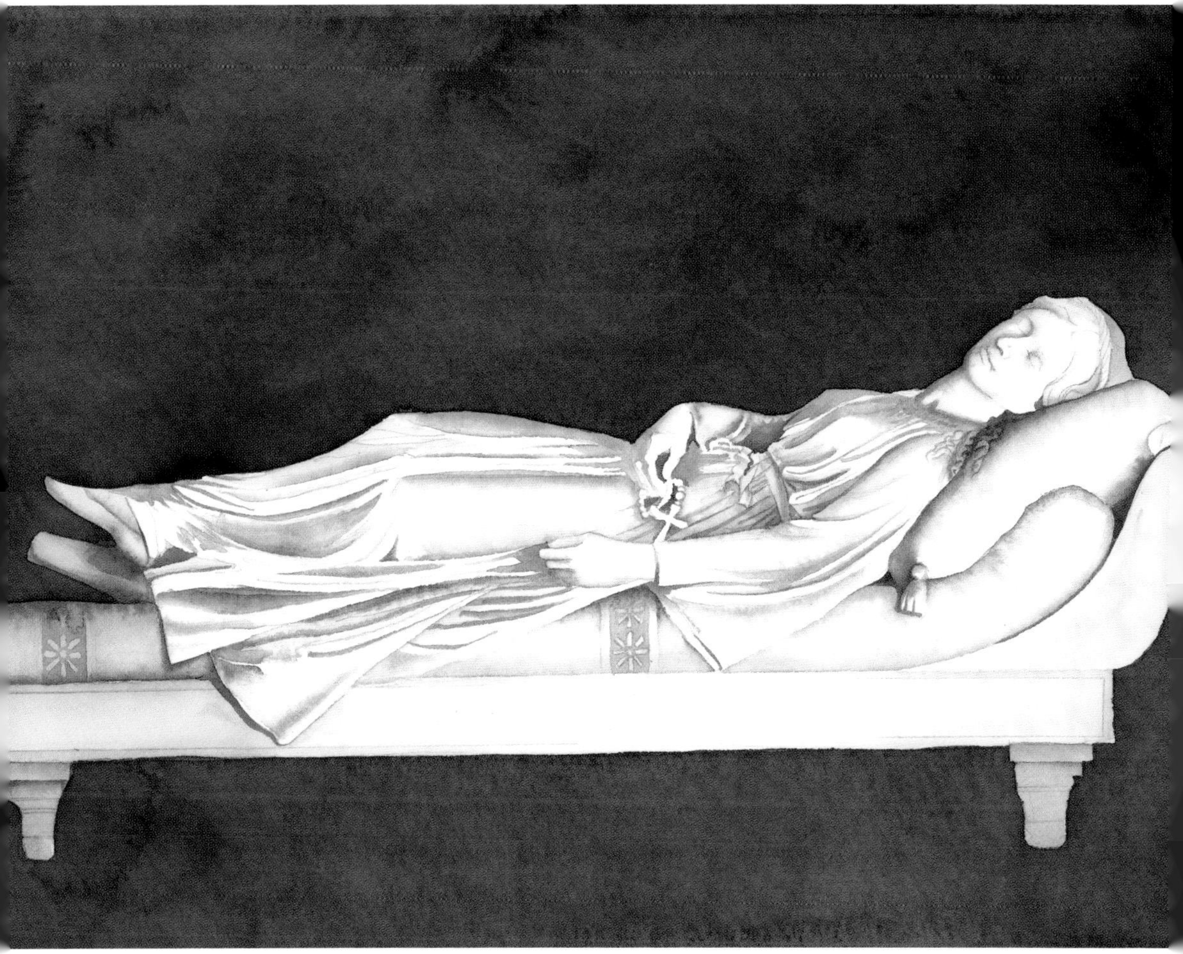

Will-o'-the-Wisp
2007 (p. 49), 2006 (p. 50), and 2007 (p. 51)
watercolor on paper, 15 x 12 in.

Will-o'-the-Wisp, 1856
Three known variations, 1856, 1858, and 1864, five known versions
Marble • 33 3/4 x 16 3/4 x 18 1/8"
Signed and inscribed (base, carved in marble): "Harriet Hosmer Roma"

Provenance

Collection
First Variation
a. *Present Owners*
1858
Signed and inscribed (base, recto): "Will-O-The-Wisp"
(base, verso) "HARRIET HOSMER FECIT-ROMA"
Chrysler Museum, Norfolk, VA
Gift of James H. Ricau and Museum Purchase, 1986
86.472
Previous Owners
Private Collection, New York, NY
Raymond's Antiques, Alexandria, VA, 1970
Giacomo P. d'Avanzo, 1971
Skinner's Bolton, MA, 1982
Hirschl & Adler Galleries, New York, NY, 1982
Private Collection, 1984
James H. Ricau, Piermont, NY, 1984
b. *Present Owners*
1858
32 1/2 x 16 3/4 x 17"
Signed and inscribed (base, verso): "HARRIET HOSMER FECIT ROMAE"
Smithsonian American Art Museum, Washington, D.C.
Museum Purchase, 1987
Previous Owners
Daniel B. Grossman, Inc. Fine Art, New York, NY
Robert W. Skinner Galleries, Bolton, MA
Collection Eloise Green, MA
Collection Clark L. Green, Ashby, MA
c. *Present Owners*
Signed and inscribed (base, recto): "Will-O-The-Wisp"
Watertown Free Public Library, Watertown, MA
Gift of Watertown Library Trustees and Friends, 1992
Second Variation
d. *Present Owners*
1856
Previously known as "Baby Faun and Owl" and "Puck and the Owl"
35 1/2 x 21 1/2 x 15 1/4"
Boston Athenaeum, Boston, MA, 1876
UH22
Previous Owners
Hannah F. (Sawyer) Lee, Boston, MA
Julia Bryant (Mrs. Charles J.) Paine, Boston, MA
Third Variation
e. *Present Owners*
1864
31 7/8 x 17 3/8 x 23 1/4"
Signed and inscribed (base, recto): "Will-O-The-Wisp"
Chrysler Museum, Norfolk, VA
Gift of James H. Ricau and Museum Purchase, 1986
86.472
Previous Owners
Elmo Avet, New Orleans, LA
James H. Ricau, Piermont, NY, 1986
Exhibitions
The Annual Exhibition of Paintings and Statuary, at the Athenaeum Gallery. Boston Athenaeum, Boston, MA, 1866, 1867
A Climate for Art. Boston Athenaeum, Boston, MA, 1980
Lines of A Different Character: American Art from 1727 to 1947. Hirschl & Adler Galleries, New York, NY, 1982–1983
Images of Innocence: The Child in American Art. Smithsonian American Art Museum, Washington, D.C., 1987–1990
The Ricau Collection. The Chrysler Museum, Norfolk, VA, 1989
Young America: Treasures from the Smithsonian American Art Museum. TOUR, Smithsonian American Art Museum, Washington, D.C., 2000–2003

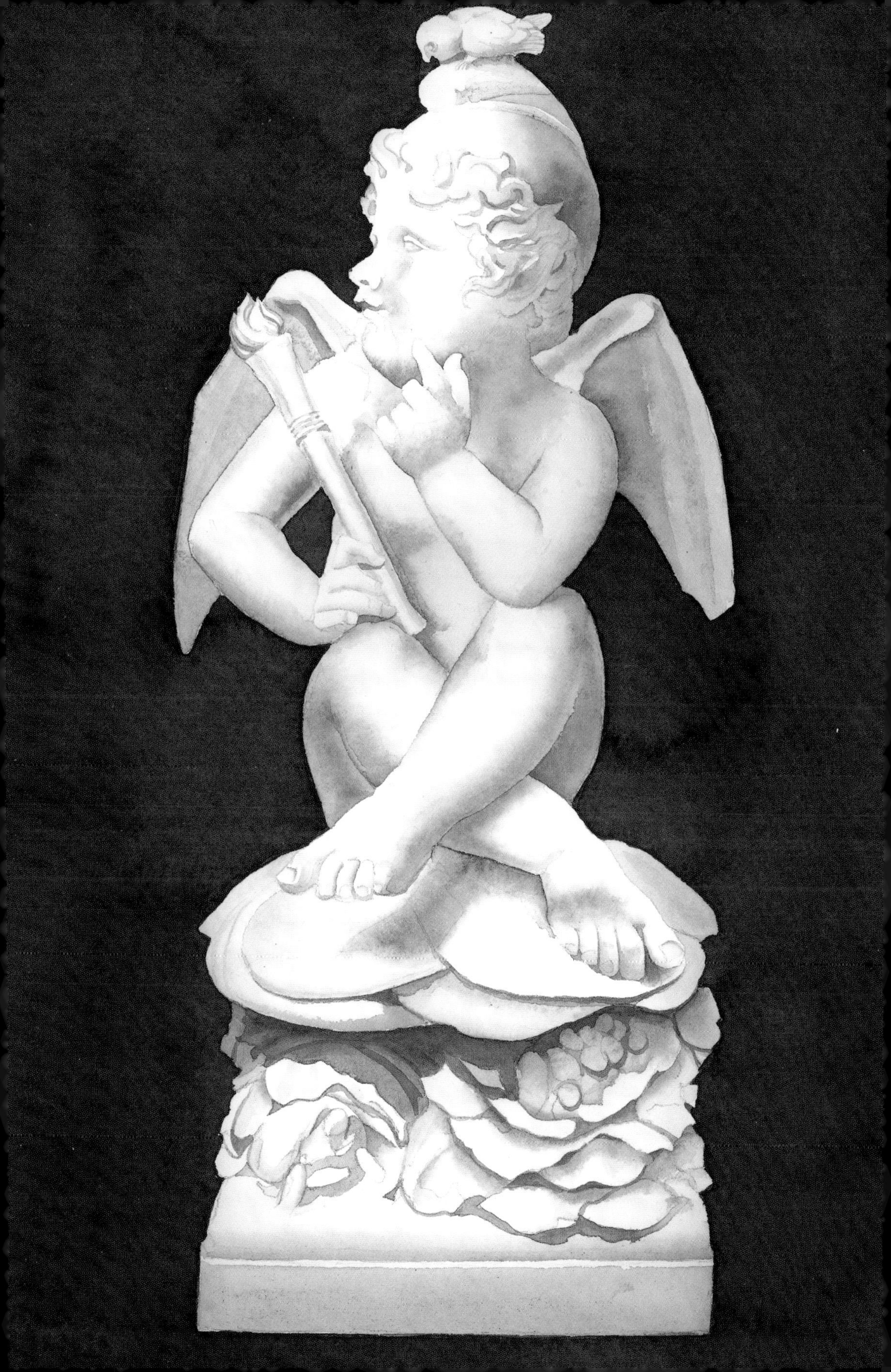

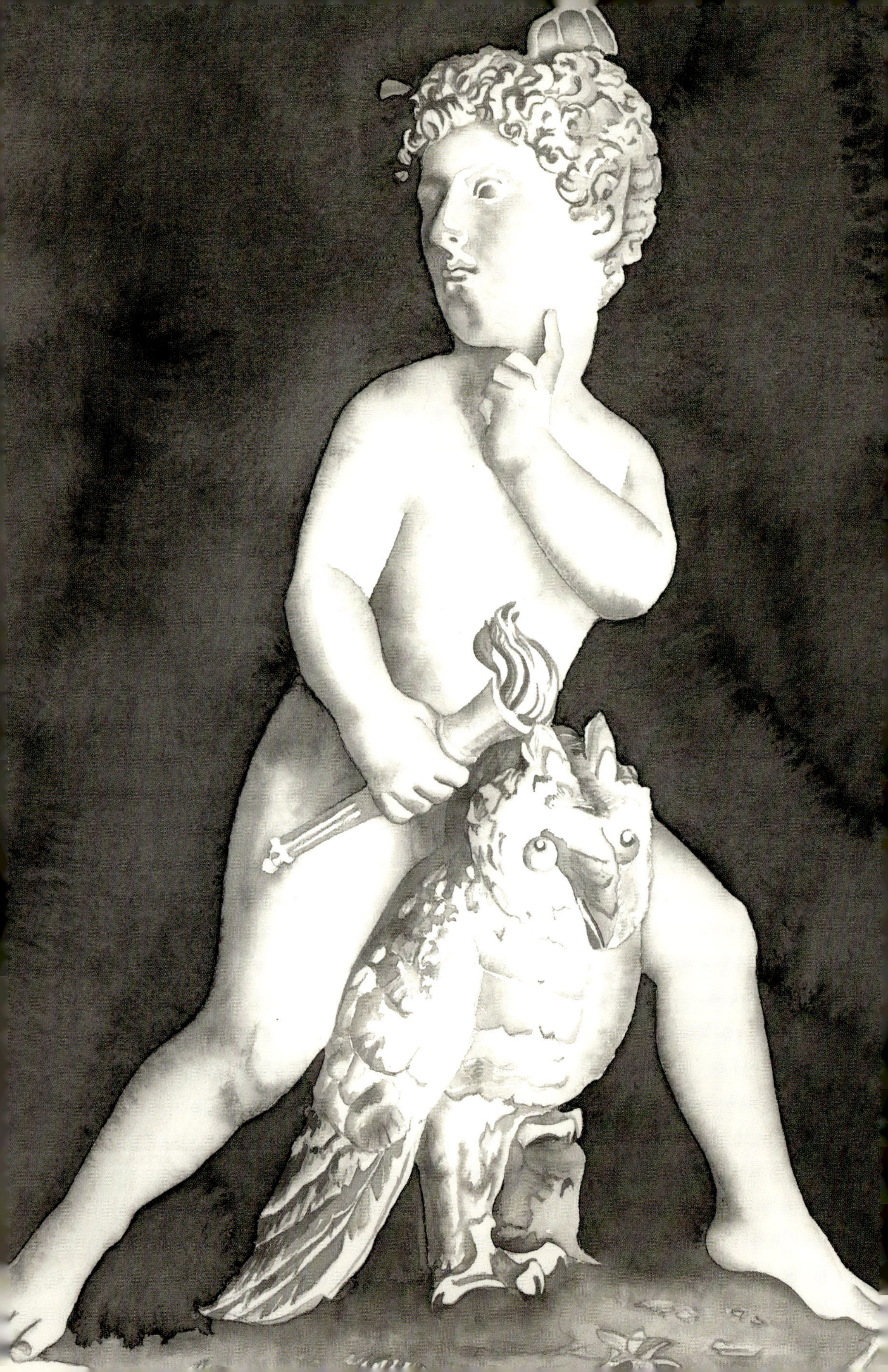

Seen But Not Heard: Images of Children from the Collection of the Boston Athenaeum. Boston Athenaeum, Boston, MA, 2004
Acquired Tastes: 200 Years of Collecting for the Boston Athenaeum. Boston Athenaeum, Boston, MA, 2007

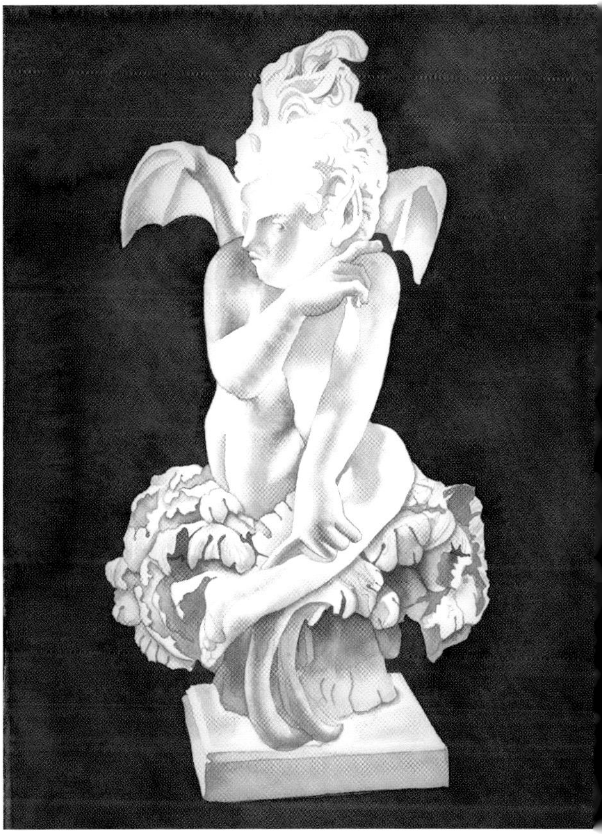

The second of Hosmer's *fancy pieces*, *Will-o'-the-Wisp*, was made as a companion for her very successful *Puck*. Also inspired by Shakespeare's *A Midsummer Night's Dream*, Will is a marshland fairy who could adopt a phosphorescent glow and had a habit of scaring lost travelers.
Hosmer created three variations on this theme.
In the first variation, the cherubic winged sprite sits on a skunk cabbage patch. The turtle below references the swampy home. The torch he holds and the owl a top his head reference his nocturnal habits.
In the second variation, Hosmer inverts the previous forms. The little baby has grown up into a young child, the cabbage patch has disappeared and been replaced with a large owl which he straddles. The scale shift creates an uneasy juxtaposition. The previously large bat wings have shrunken and moved onto his curly head. The torch is now lowered and seems less threatening.
It seems Hosmer wasn't satisfied with the second design because in the third variation she returned to abundant foliage supporting Will, this time robust acanthus leaves. Will still has the baby's body, his streamlined facial features appear more specific and less ideal. The torch has been replaced by a swirl of hair coifed into flames, and the large bat wings have returned to his back. He looks to the right and points to the left as if he just spied his next victim. He is poised to swing into action. The variety of foliage and range of textures gives Hosmer an opportunity to exhibit her virtuosic carving skills.
Although *Will-o'-the-Wisp*, all three variations, never duplicated the critical or financial success of *Puck*, Hosmer explored a more complex character, one slightly malevolent in nature.

The Fountain of the Hylas and the Water Nymphs

2007
watercolor on paper, 15 x 12 in.

The Fountain of the Hylas and the Water Nymphs, 1858
Marble • Height: unknown
Signed and inscribed (verso): unknown

Provenance

Collection
Present Owners
Probably destroyed
Previous Owners
Unknown
Exhibitions
None, it was a domestic commission

Female sculptors seem to have been commissioned most frequently to create domestic architectural elements (fountains, gates, and fireplace mantles) for aristocratic homes. One of the most famous fountains of the time was *Angel of the Waters*, otherwise known as Bethesda Fountain, in Central Park, created in 1871. Not so famous is the name of the artist who made it, Hosmer's friend, Emma Stebbins.

Hosmer designed four fountains.

The Fountain of the Hylas and the Water Nymphs was the first in 1858, *The Fountain of the Siren* was second in 1861, and *The Triton* and its companion, *The Mermaid's Cradle*, in 1892. They were realized in stone and bronze.

No photograph of the work survives. Its location is unknown and it is thought to have been destroyed. It was recorded to still be in Hosmer's studio in 1861. In Bolton's *Lives of Girls Who Became Famous* it is described as a work with "dolphins sprouting jets on the lower basin, and a youthful Hylas in the upper, surrounded by the admiring nymphs who would soon draw him into the water and drown him."

Hosmer would utilize dolphin imagery in other fountain designs. These water mammals, with their graceful leaps and playful splashing, seem appropriate subjects for lavish fountains. But, in Greek and Roman Mythology they had another meaning. Dolphins were spirits who guided souls to the underworld and paradise.

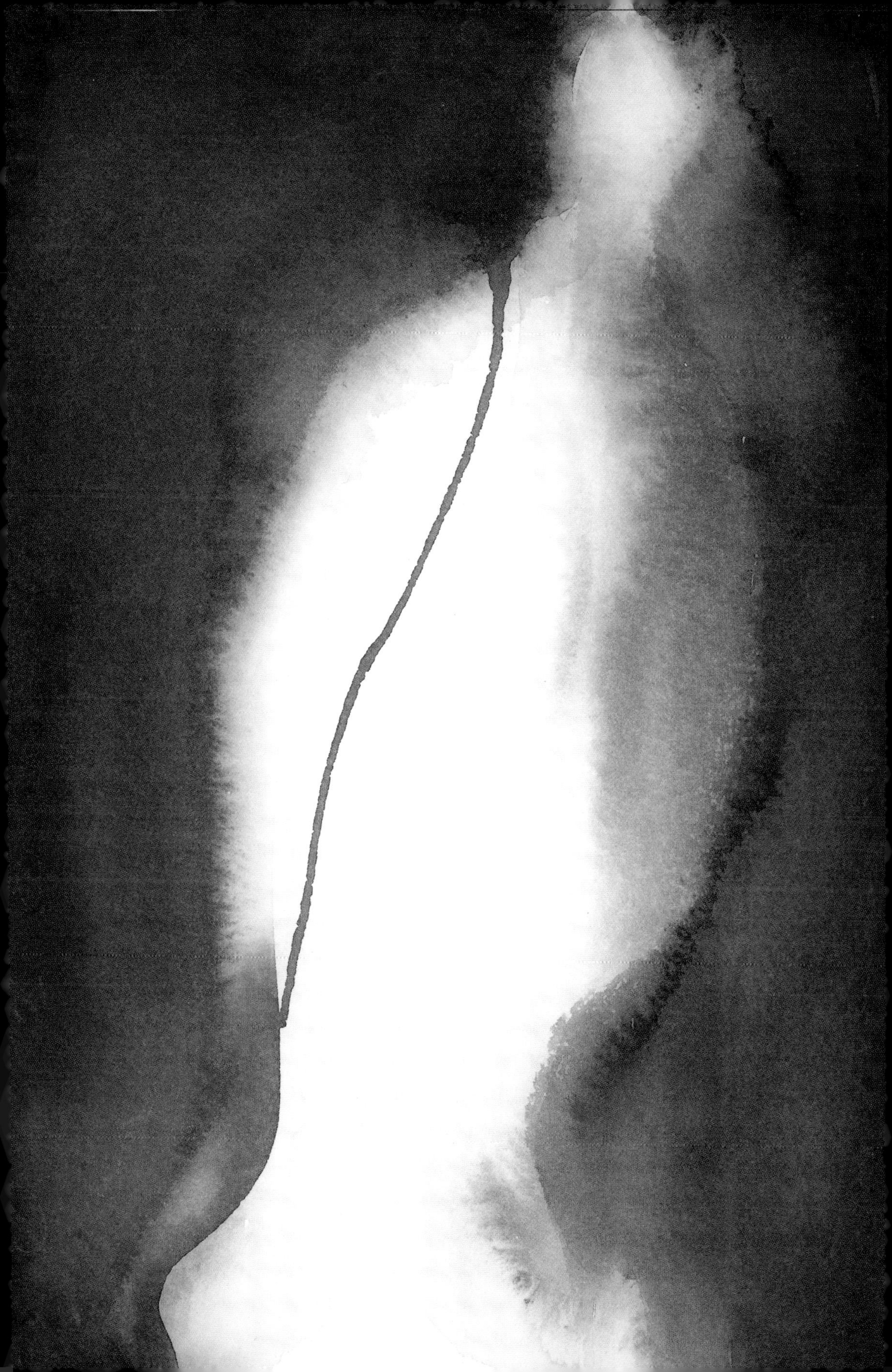

Zenobia

2007

watercolor on paper, 15 x 12 in.

Zenobia, 1859

Four known versions (full size, 2/3rd size, full size bust, 2/3rd bust, possibly eight)

Marble • 82 x 26 1/2 x 31"

Signed and inscribed (carved base, verso): "HARRIET HOSMER ME SCULPSIT ROMAE"

Provenance

Collection

a. *Present Owners*
   Full figure version
   Huntington Library, Art Collections, and Botanical Gardens, San Marino, CA
   Purchased with funds from the Virginia Steele Scott Foundation
   2007.26
   Previous Owners
   Mr. Almon Griswold, New York, NY, 1864
   Sotheby's, London, 2007

b. *Present Owners*
   49 x 16 x 21"
   Signed and inscribed (on base): "Harriet Hosmer Fecit Romae"
   Wadsworth Athenaeum, Hartford, CT
   1900.8
   Previous Owners
   Mrs. Josephine M. J. Dodge, New York, NY

c. *Present Owners*
   44 1/4 x 14 x 18"
   Saint Louis Museum of Fine Arts, Saint Louis, MO
   American Art Purchase Fund
   19:2008
   Previous Owners
   Mr. Robert W. Emmons, Boston, MA

d. *Present Owners*
   34 x 22 1/5 x 12 1/3" (bust)
   Signed and inscribed (verso): "Harriet Hosmer/Fecit Romae"
   Art Institute of Chicago, Chicago, IL
   Restricted gift of the Antiquarian Society
   1993.260
   Previous Owners
   Conner-Rosenkranz, New York, NY, 1993

e. *Present Owners*
   17 x 12 x 6" (bust)
   Signed and inscribed (verso): "Harriet Hosmer/Fecit Roma"
   Watertown Free Public Library, Watertown, MA
   Gift of Harriet Hosmer Carr, 1923
   Previous Owners
   Harriet Hosmer Carr

Exhibitions
   International Exhibition, London, 1862
   Fine Art Institute, Derby Gallery, 625 Broad Street, New York, NY, 1864
   Childs and Jenks Art Gallery, Tremont Street, Boston, MA, 1864
   Sanitary Fair, Chicago, IL, 1865
   Metropolitan Museum of Art, New York, NY, 1912
   The White, Marmorean Flock: Nineteenth Century American Neoclassical Sculptors. Vassar College Art Gallery, Poughkeepsie, NY, 1972
   American Women Artists: 1830 – 1930. International Exhibitions Foundation for the National Museum of Women in the Arts, Washington, D.C. (traveled to Minneapolis Institute of Art, Minneapolis, MN; Wadsworth Athenaeum Museum of Art, Hartford, CT; San Diego Museum of Art, San Diego, CA; Meadow Museum, Dallas, TX), 1988

The first of three celebrated female sovereigns Hosmer chose to create and her first non-commissioned full-length statue was a marble statue of Zenobia, the third-century Queen of Palmyra. The statue was exhibited at the International Exhibition in London and became the focus of a slander scandal that Hosmer handled adeptly. Accused by jealous male competitors of not making the statue herself, Hosmer responded in print and in a lawsuit thus restoring her good name and artistic reputation.
Zenobia co-ruled what is now present-day Syria with her husband, King Odaenathus, until his assassination in 267. She then ruled alone in proxy for her son, conquering Egypt and much of Asia Minor. In 274, she was defeated by Roman Emperor Aurelian, taken to Rome as a war trophy, and

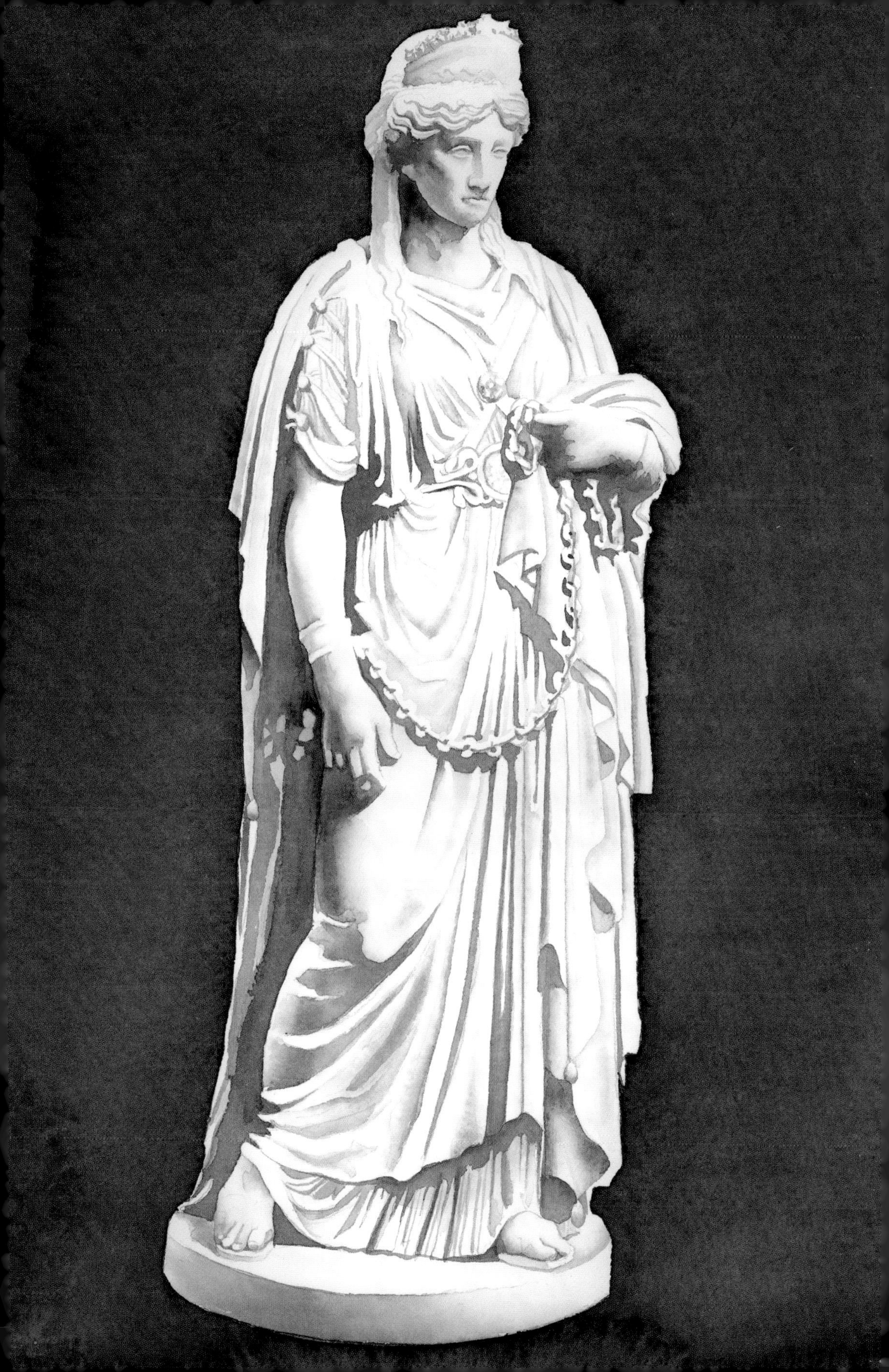

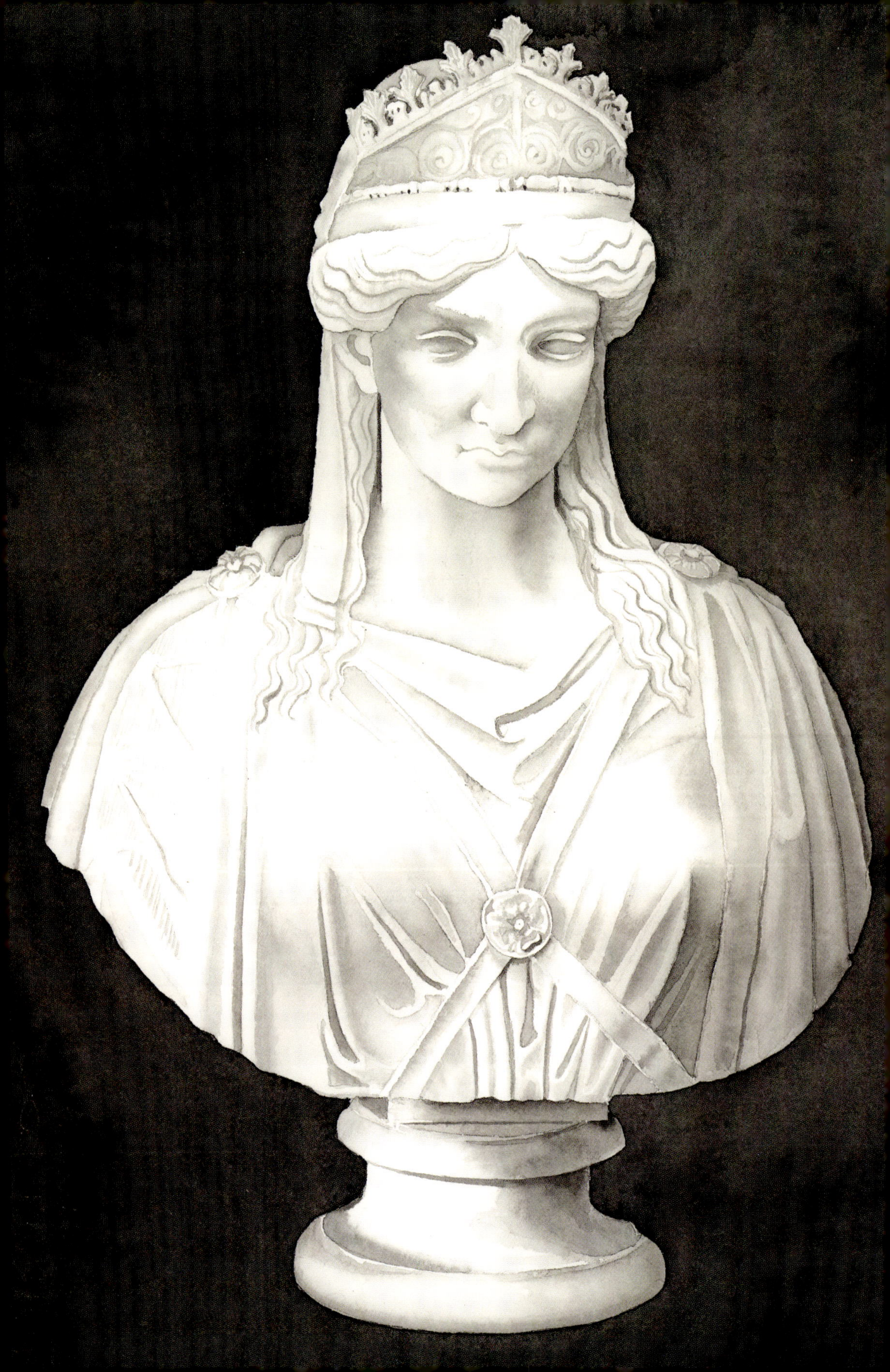

marched through the streets in chains. In contrast, when Cleopatra was defeated three centuries earlier, she committed suicide to avoid such public humiliation.

Except for one visual source, a coin with the Queen's profile that Hosmer may have seen, all the sources for the work are literary. However, Hosmer transforms the traditional treatment of Zenobia failing her people with her vanity and pride into one of courage, majesty, and dignity.

Nathaniel Hawthorne was the first to compare Hosmer's *Zenobia* to *Athena Giustinaiani* (the goddess of wisdom and war) and the Barberini *Juno* (queen of the Olympian gods) both in the Vatican Museum Collection. Hosmer's *Zenobia* is monumental, over life size, wearing the regal dress and jewels appropriate for her royal position. Her gaze is slightly lowered, her hand easily gathers copious folds of the chiton drapery. The large chains don't seem to burden her. She steps forward slowly, deliberately, her size and weight powerful, giving the subject authority and gravitas.

Although it was Zenobia who used her diplomatic skills to avoid death, remarry, have several more children and live out her life comfortably in Tivoli, it is Cleopatra who remained a popular subject for male artists for centuries. Hosmer's alternate choice of Zenobia as a powerful female leader is unique and demonstrates her growing interest in the position of women in the world.

The Fountain of the Siren
2007
watercolor on paper, 15 x 12 in.

The Fountain of the Siren (including *Putti upon Dolphin*), 1861
Marble • 7' height (putti height 33")
Signed and inscribed (verso): unknown

Provenance

Collection
Present Owners
Destroyed, 2 Putti upon Dolphin fragments survive
The Marquess of Northampton, Northampton, England
Previous Owners
Lady Marion Alford
Alford House at Prince's Gate, London, England

This is the most well known of Hosmer's fountain designs. She made two versions. This one was commissioned by Lady Marion Alford, her lover and the oldest daughter of the 2nd Marquess of Northampton. She was paid a reported $12,500 for the fountain. It was installed in the fountain room of Alford House, a single story room with an octagonal glass dome. Lady Alford used the house as her London residence from 1872 to 1887. The building was demolished in 1931 and it is believed that the fountain was destroyed. The second one was installed in the courtyard of Hosmer's Roman studio. Its whereabouts are unknown.
The elaborate marble fountain was over 7' high. At the top of the design sits the *Song of the Siren* holding a reed pipe she raises as if about to play. She is perched upon three beautiful shells that form a basin from which flowed water creating the only audible "music."
The ornately carved vertical pedestal that supported the shells was encircled by three *Putti upon Dolphin* on the lower level. The Putti are chubby water amorini reminiscent of Hosmer's popular *Puck*. They ride animated dolphins like bucking broncos. Their heads tilted back in glee and also so that they can hear the Siren above them. Only two *Putti upon Dolphin* exist today.
The lower hexagonal shape has a turtle at each corner. A sculptural precedent is the *Turtle Fountain* (1581) designed by Giacomo della Porta in Piazza Mattei in Rome which Hosmer certainly would have known. The turtles on this fountain are attributed to Gian Lorenzo Bernini.
Hosmer reinscribes the playful aspects of her fancy pieces in her fountain designs possibly to counterbalance her more independent depictions of women. The fountain installed in the courtyard entrance to Hosmer's Roman studio must have made a big impression on the visitors of the Grand Tour.

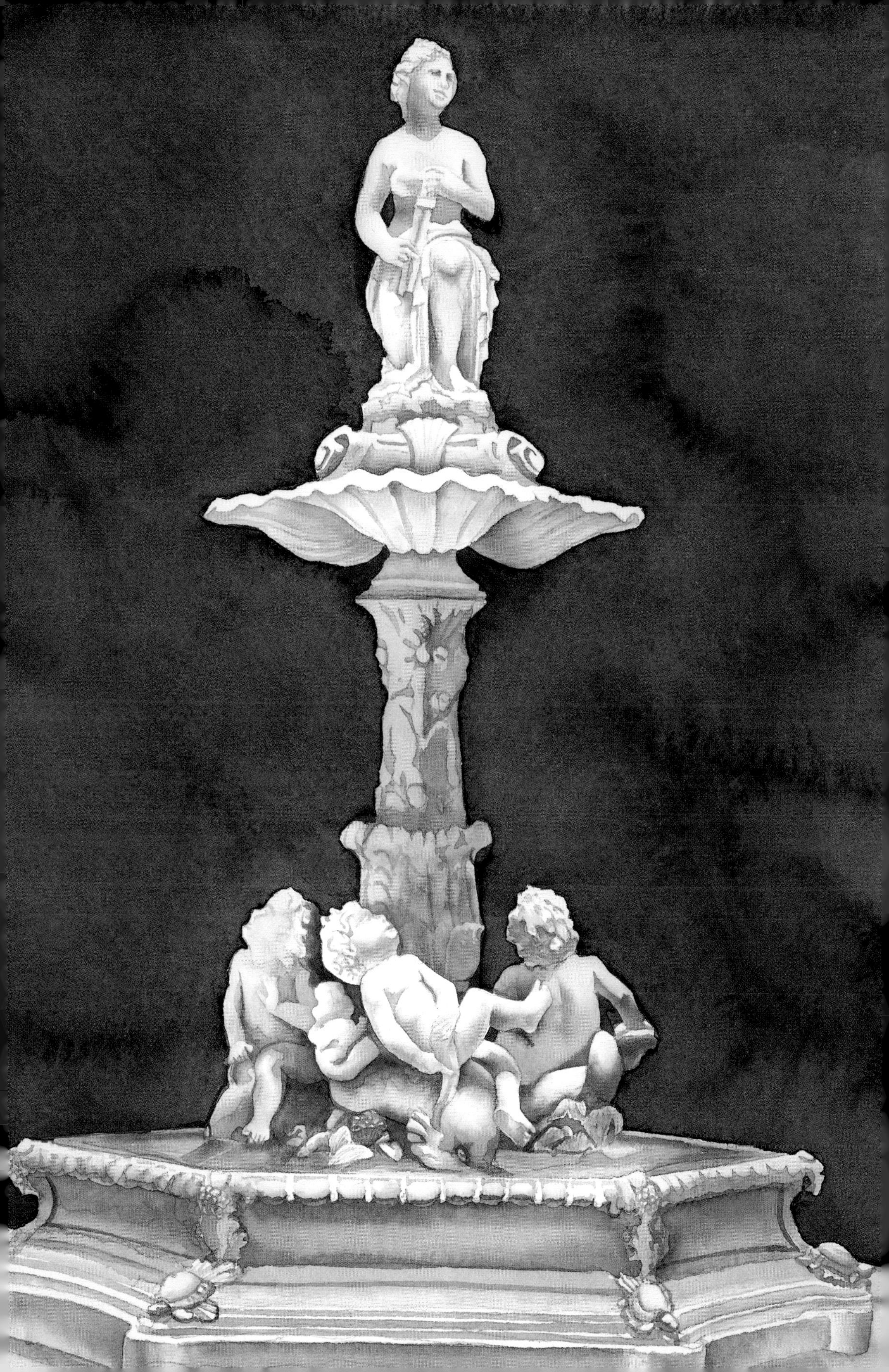

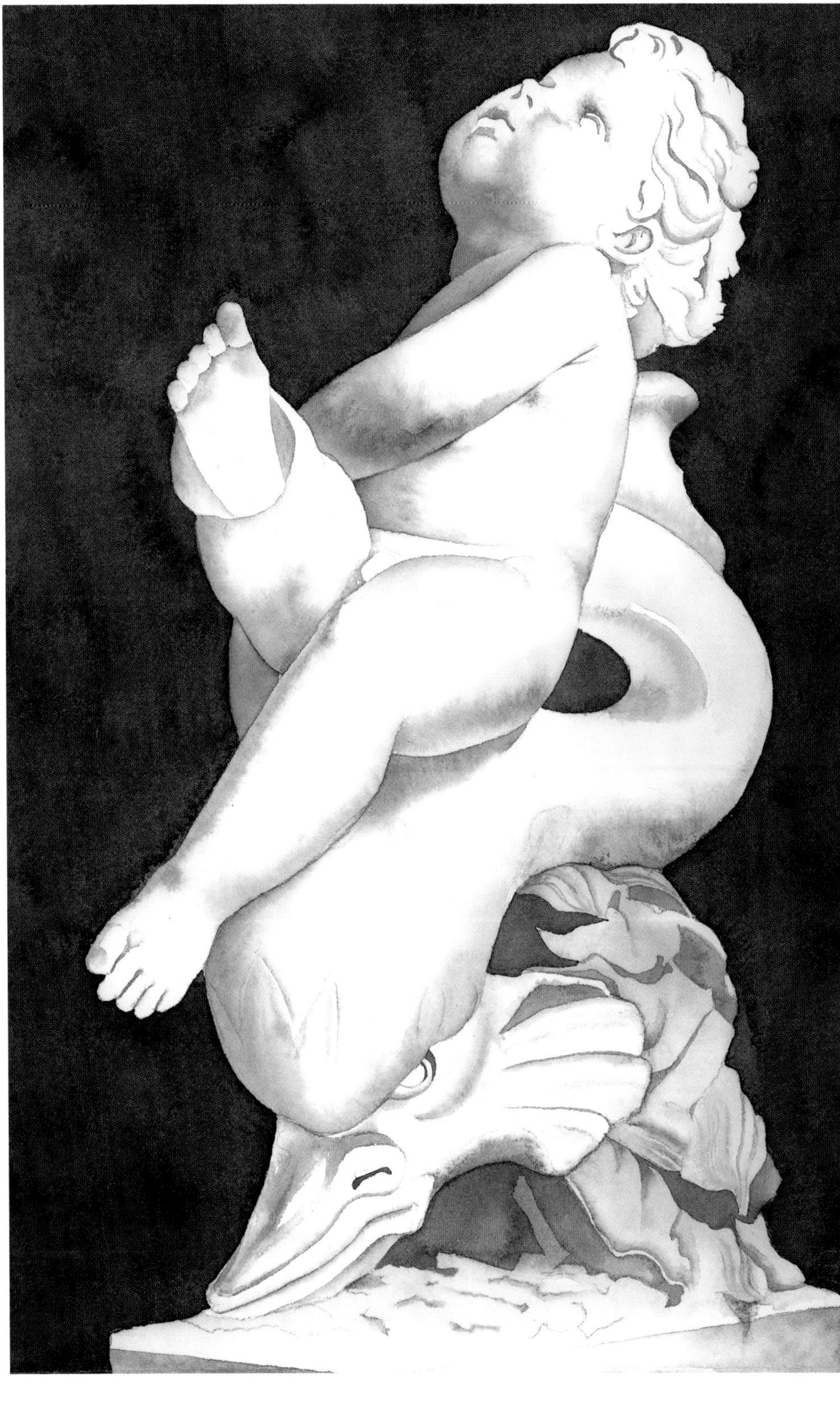

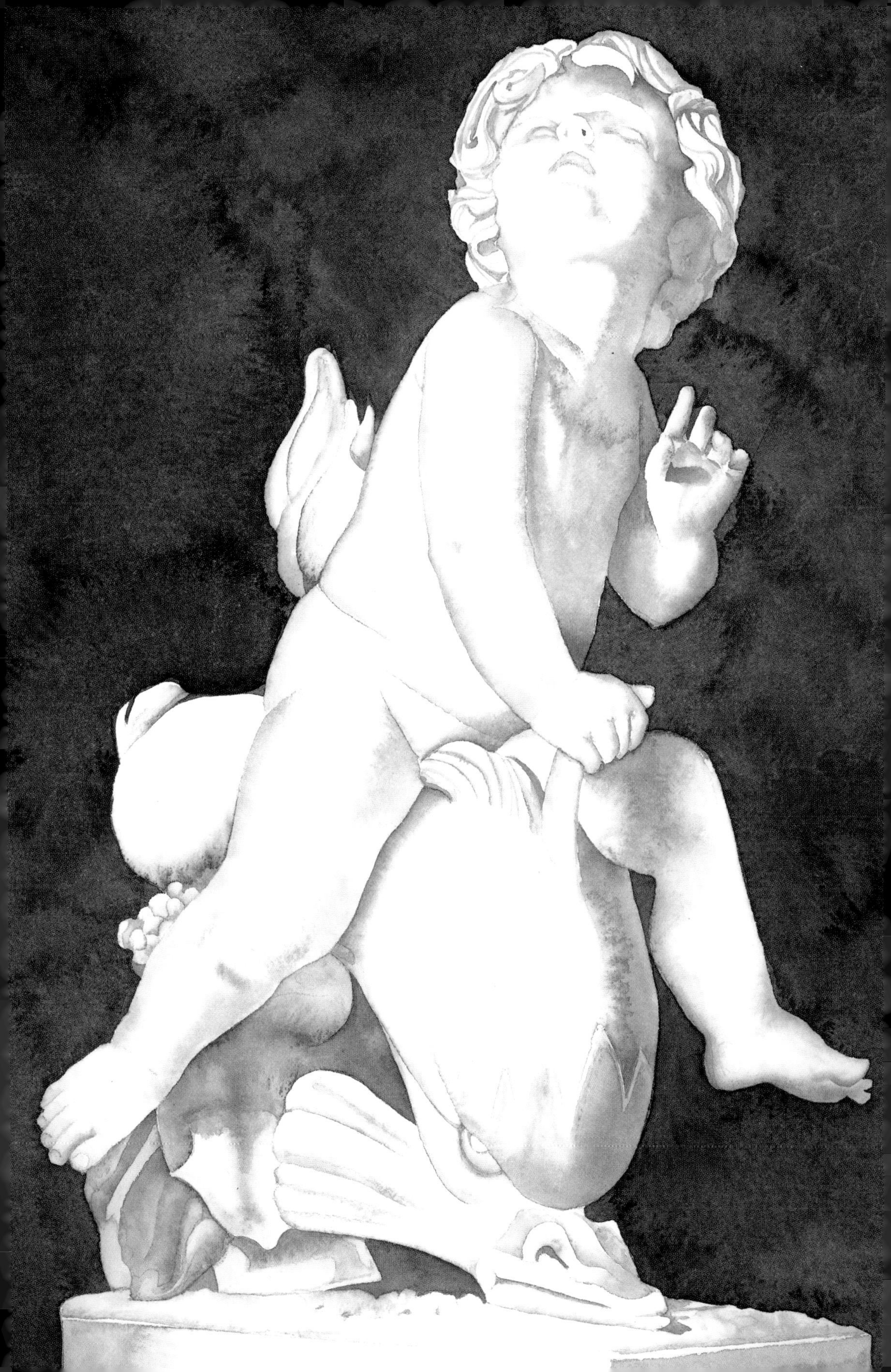

Thomas Hart Benton
2007
watercolor on paper, 15 x 12 in.

Thomas Hart Benton, 1862 (dedicated 1868)
Bronze • 10' height • Base 13' h x 10' 7"
Signed and dated (verso): "Harriet Hosmer Fecit Roma"
Inscribed (recto): "There is the East, there is India"

Provenance

Collection
Present Owners
Lafayette Park, St. Louis, MO

Hosmer made three full-length male statues: first, the monumental bronze statue *Thomas Hart Benton* (1862, dedicated 1868), then *The Sleeping Faun* (1864–1865), followed by its companion, *The Waking Faun* (1866–1867).

Senator Thomas Benton was the first public monument in the state of Missouri. It was commissioned by the City of St. Louis for Lafayette Park, where it still stands. The competition for the commission was fierce and winning it was a huge professional victory for Hosmer. Wayman Crow, Hosmer's staunch supporter, was on the selection committee. It was cast in bronze at the Royal Foundry in Munich, where all the expatriate sculptors had their work cast in the nineteenth century. She received $30,000 for the commission of which $20,000 was spent on fabrication, which was a fortune then.

Senator Thomas Hart Benton (1782–1858) was a Missouri senator for thirty years. A great expansionist, he encouraged citizens to settle the west by selling them land cheaply.

A possible visual source for the statue is the Roman statue of *Demosthenes* in the Vatican Museum Collection which Hosmer certainly would have known. Both *Demosthenes* and *Benton* are draped in the folds of an antique cloak, wear sandal-like boots, and place all their weight on one leg. Both men hold a piece of paper. Demosthenes, the orator, opens a scroll, while Benton, the expansionist, unfurls a map of North America. The only visible trace of modernity in Hosmer's piece is an ascot-like collar and cuffs of a shirt that peak out from under the drapery. Benton's face is not idealized. It is a portrait. He looks down, thick waves of hair framing his benevolent face.

Hosmer's choice to dress Senator Benton in classical garb subscribes to the tenants of neo-classicism, harking back to the senators of ancient Greece and linking our national statesmen with the wisdom and bravery of the Ancients. This is Hosmer's first public depiction of a male subject after building her reputation for skillfully depicting feminine sensuality and grace. It was professionally advantageous that she prove she could do both.

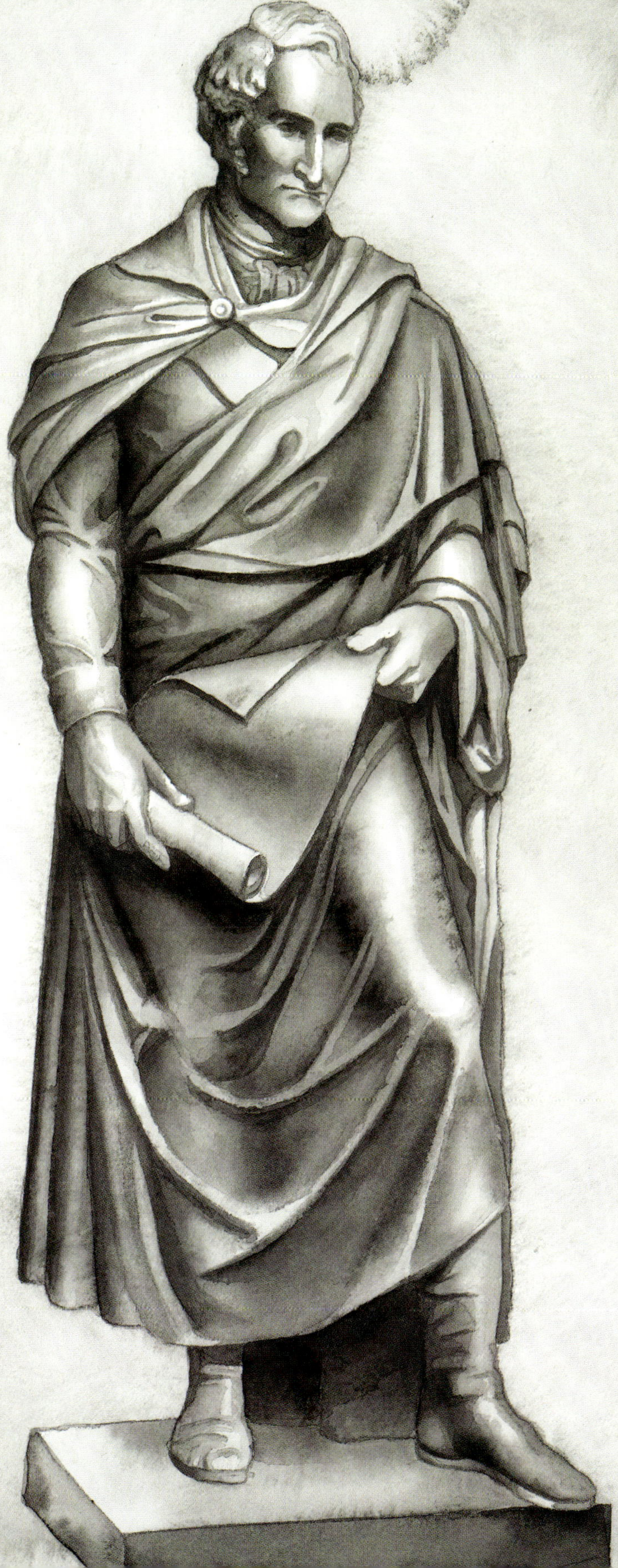

Gate For An Art Gallery

2007

watercolor on paper, 12 x 15 in.

Gate For An Art Gallery, 1864
Graphite on paper • Size unknown
Location unknown
Photograph of the design in Watertown Library

Exhibitions
Probably none. It was a domestic commission and might not have been completed

a. *Night Rises with the Stars*
1856
Marble bas-relief
Medallion 16" diameter
In gilt wood frame
27 x 35"
Signed and dated (verso): unknown
PROVENANCE
Collection
Present Owners
Bigelow Chapel of Mount Auburn Cemetery, Watertown, MA
Previous Owners
Unknown

b. *Phospher and Hesper Circling their Double Star*
1856
Marble bas-relief
Medallion 16" diameter
Signed and dated (verso): unknown
PROVENANCE
Collection
Present Owners
Unknown
Previous Owners
Unknown

c. *The Falling Star*
Date unknown
Marble bas-relief
Medallion 16" diameter
Signed and dated (verso): unknown
PROVENANCE
Collection
Present Owners
Unknown
Previous Owners
Unknown

d. *Zepher Descends*
(date unknown)
Marble bas-relief
Medallion 16" diameter
Signed and dated (verso): unknown
PROVENANCE
Collection
Present Owners
Unknown
Previous Owners
Unknown

Very little is known about Hosmer's *Gate For An Art Gallery*. Hosmer's lover, Lady Marion Alford, lived at Ashridge Hall, Berkhamsted, Hertfordshire, England and it is most likely that her son, Earl Brownlow, commissioned the design for a reported $25,000.

The Gates were never completed. But, based on a photograph of the sketch and photographs of four of the marble bas relief medallions in the Watertown Free Public Library, it appears that it was to be 16 feet tall and almost 10 feet wide. It was an elaborate design, with a dozen bas relief medallions, four oblong oval reliefs, two lunettes, and a reigning nude male angel below the top arch.

The theme is the twelve hours of night. They are: Eolus Subdues The Winds, Zephyr Borne To The Earth, Iris Descends With The Dew, Night Rises With The Stars, The Hours Sleep, The Moon Rises, The Dreams Descend, The Falling Star, Phospher And Hesper, The Hours Awake, Aurora Veils The Stars, and Morning. The oblong reliefs at the bottom are believed to be Centaurs and Wood Nymphs, and Tritons and Sea Nymphs. Only one of those marbles, *Night Rises with the Stars*, can be located today.

Hosmer's interest in mythological subjects was constant throughout her career. Perhaps the myths surrounding night and sleep resonated so strongly with her because they metaphorically addressed the issue of death. Night, as a subject for doors to an art gallery, is curious. Is that when inspiration came to her or when she had peace?

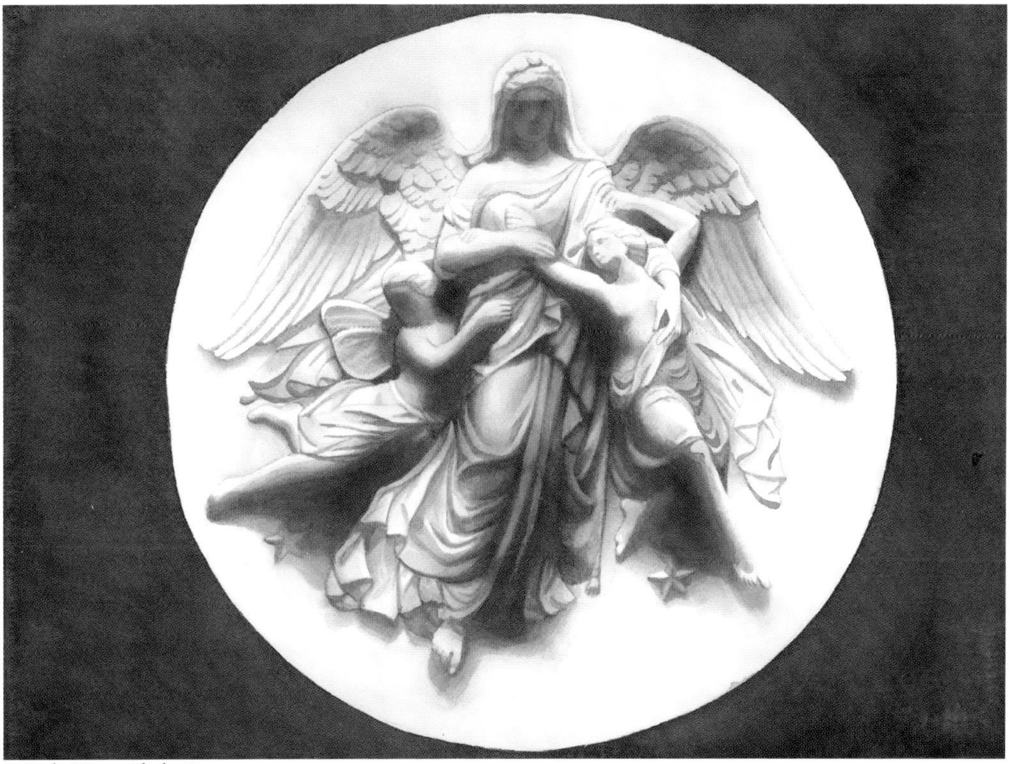

a. *Night Rises with the Stars*

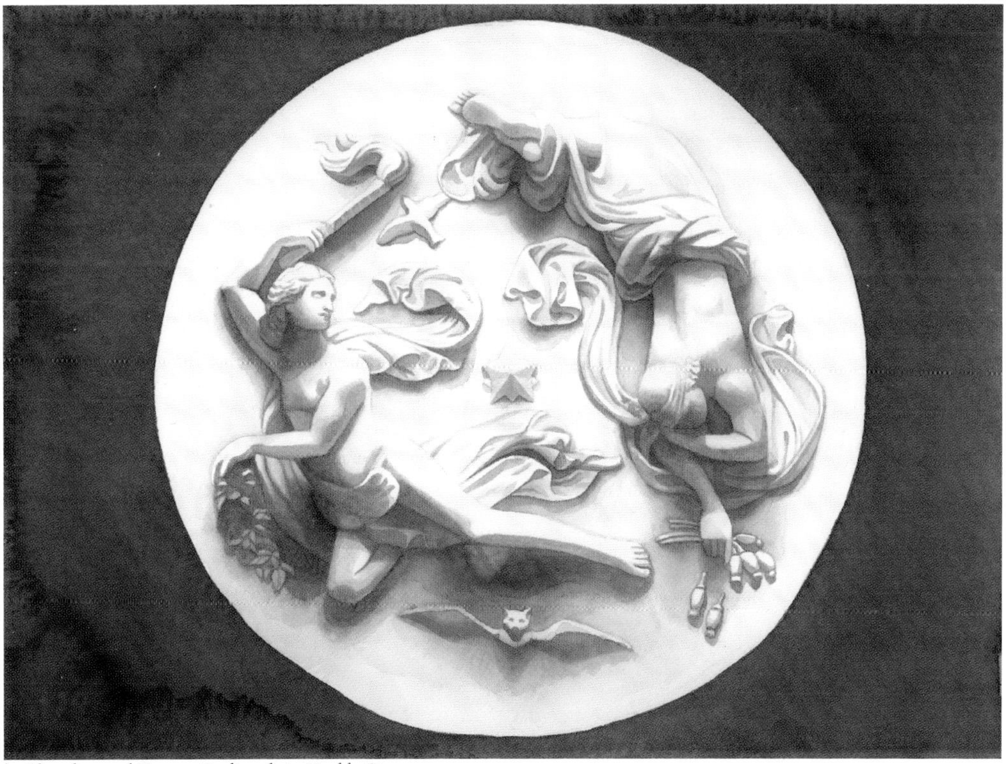

b. *Phospher and Hesper Circling their Double Star*

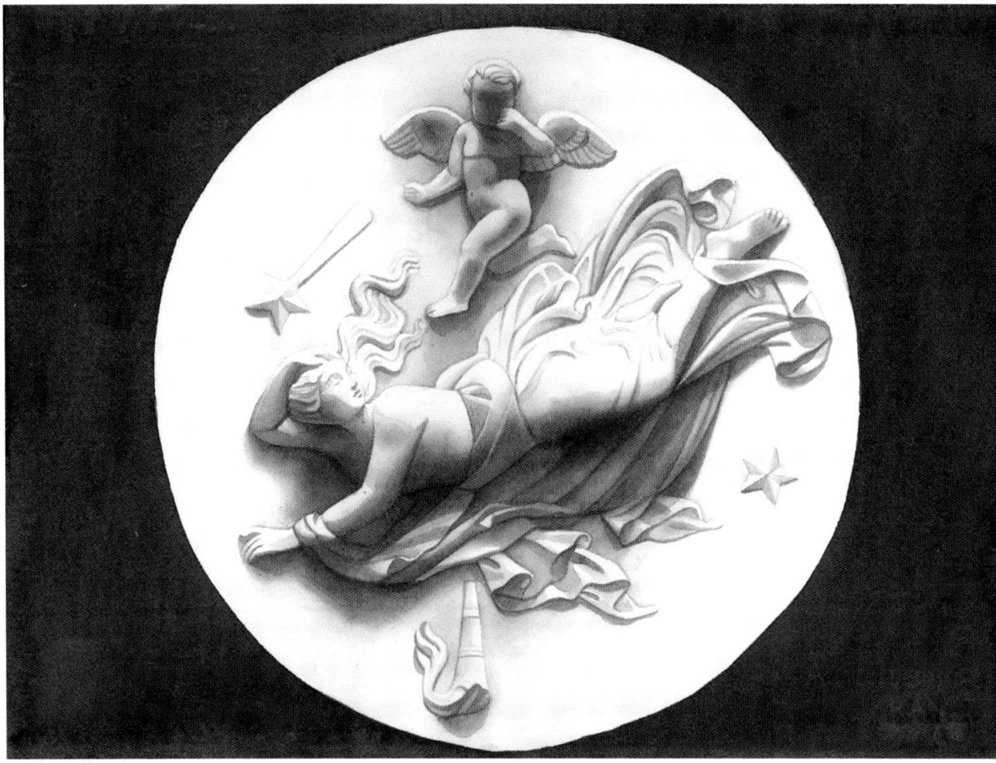

c. *The Falling Star*

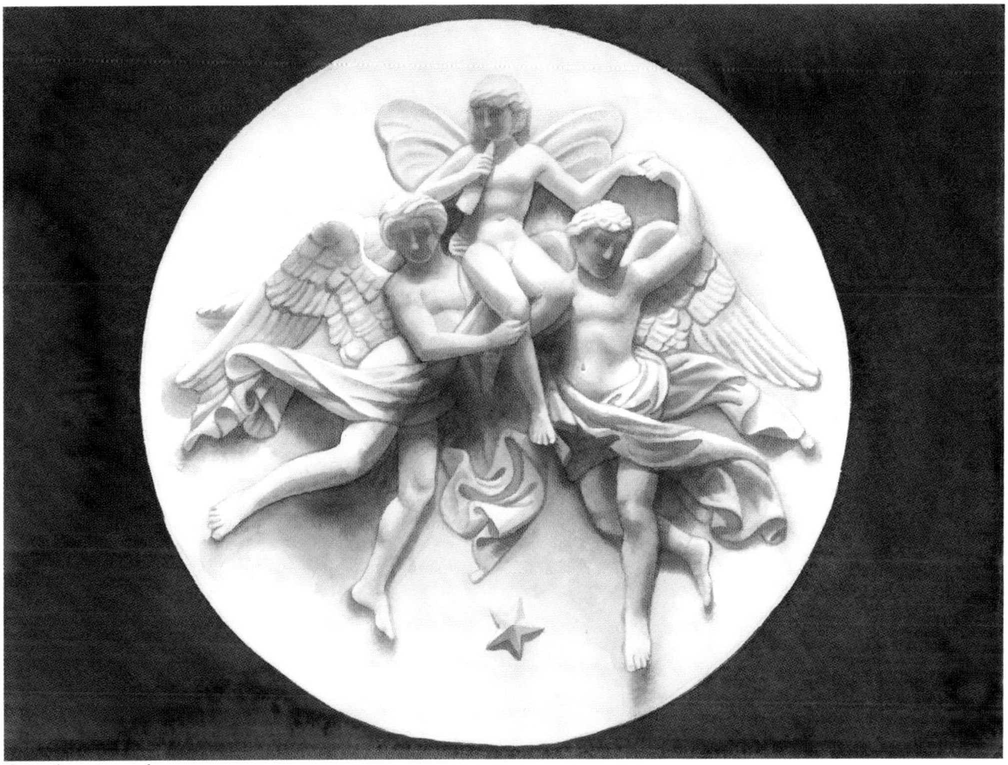

d. *Zepher Descends*

The Sleeping Faun
2006
watercolor on paper, 12 x 15 in.

The Sleeping Faun, 1864, 1865 (modeled date, carved date)
Four known versions (possibly eight versions)
Marble • 49 x 60"
Signed and inscribed (verso): "HARRIET HOSMER Fecit - Romae"
Inscribed base (recto): "The Sleeping Faun"

Provenance

Collection
a. *Present Owners*
Deptartment of Foreign Affairs, Dublin, Ireland
Gift of Sir Benjamin Guinness, 1866
Previous Owners
Sir Benjamin Guinness
b. *Present Owners*
1876
50 x 60"
Signed and inscribed (verso): "H HOSMER FECIT – ROMAE"
(base, recto): "THE SLEEPING FAUN"
Cleveland Museum of Art, Cleveland, OH
Leonard C. Hanna Jr. Fund
1997.15
Previous Owners
Prince of Wales (afterwards Edward VII), about 1876
Jacob Wakefield; Kendal Museum, Kendal, England
Sotheby's, London, England, 1977
The Forbes Magazine Collection, New York, NY
Hirschl & Adler Galleries, Inc., New York, NY, 1996
c. *Present Owners*
After 1865
34 1/2 x 41 x 16 1/2"
Signed and inscribed (verso base): "HARRIET HOSMER FECIT ROMAE"
(base, recto) "THE SLEEPING FAUN"
Museum of Fine Arts, Boston, MA
Gift of Mrs. Lucien Carr
12.709
Previous Owners
Mrs. Lucien Carr, Cambridge, MA

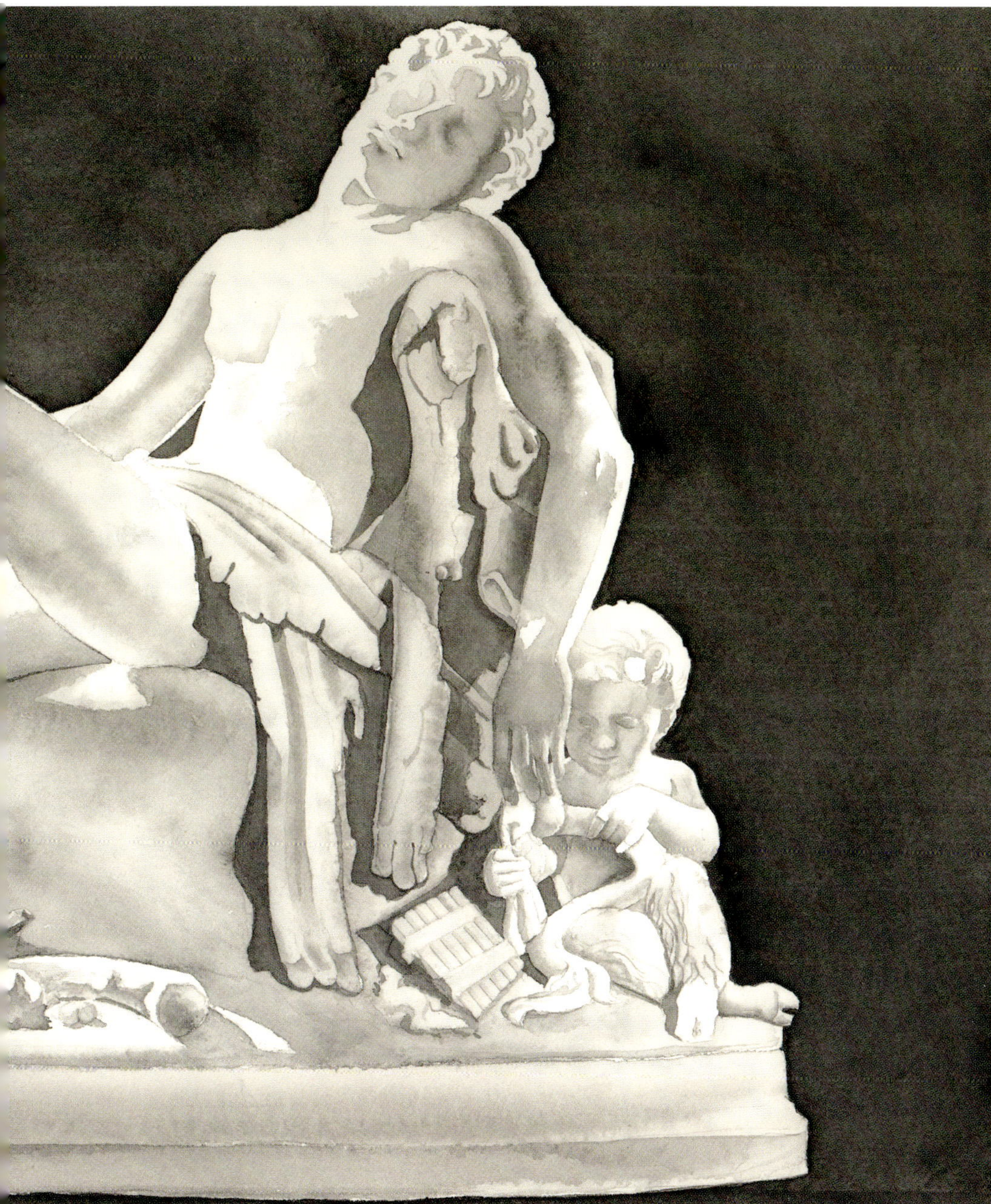

d. *Present Owners*
Destroyed, fragments survive
The Marquess of Northampton, Northampton, England
Previous Owners
Lady Ashburton
e. *Present Owners*
Destroyed, fragments survive
Dr. and Mrs. William H. Gerdts, New York, NY
Previous Owners
Mrs. Laurence C. Andrew, Portland, ME
Edward Perry Warren Estate

Exhibitions
Dublin Exhibition of 1865, Dublin, 1865
Paris Exhibition of 1867, Paris, 1867
Confident America. Museum of Fine Arts, Boston, MA, 1972
The Lure of Italy. Museum of Fine Arts, Boston, MA, (traveled to: Cleveland Museum of Art, Cleveland, OH, Museum of Fine Arts, Houston, Houston, TX), 199–1993
The Art Museum, Princeton University, Princeton, NJ, 1989–1996
Masetá di Roma da Napoleon all'Unità d'Italia. Scuderie del Quirinale, Rome, 2003

The Sleeping Faun is the second full-length male statue by Hosmer. It was exhibited in the Dublin Exhibition of 1865 and was an immediate success. A Dublin newspaper reported: "It is universally admired, and is more frequently the subject of conversation than any other statue in the exhibition."[1] It sold on the opening day to Sir Benjamin Guinness for $5,000.

The faun in Roman Mythology (like the satyr in Greek Mythology) was a half human and half goat woodland spirit, who worshiped Bacchus (Roman) or Dionysus (Greek), the god of wine. They usually had visible animal traits: tails, horns, pointed ears, hooves, and/or furry legs. Often fauns resembled a goat from the waist down and a human from the waist up.

Art historians have cited *The Barberini Faun* (220 BCE), also known as *The Drunken Faun*, in the Glyptothek collection, in Munich, Germany, as an influence. The subject of the inebriated faun, nude, sleeping against a tree, with his head lolling backwards, has similarities to Hosmer's *Faun*. To our modern eyes he seems overtly homoerotic, with legs spread in abandon with one arm stretched up behind his back. Although Hosmer didn't travel to Munich before sculpting her faun she would have known about this famous work from sketches.

A more probable influence was the *Faun of Praxiteles* (fourth century BCE) in the Capitoline Museum, in Rome. Praxiteles, the most famous of the Attic sculptors, was the ideal model for the nineteenth-century cult of Antiquity. John Gibson and Hosmer would have studied his work carefully. And not only did Nathaniel Hawthorne describe the *Faun of Praxiteles* in detail in *The Marble Faun* (1860), he also based one of the four main characters, Hilda, on Hosmer.

In Hosmer's sculpture, the Faun is also peacefully sleeping seated in semi-repose against a tree stump. In keeping with neo-classical modesty his legs are not spread wide apart like *The Barberini Faun*. Instead, he casually rests an ankle upon the opposite knee with a tiger skin draped across his lap covering his genitals. He is passive yet seductive. All the muscles in the Faun's torso, arms, and legs are relaxed, even limp. While the unsuspecting Faun sleeps, a satyr industriously ties him to the tree stump. The tension between the proximity of the satyr's active hands to the Faun's passive one, amplifies the effect of the prank. Accessories of sylvan living lie on the mossy forest floor. The grapes, flute, and bones would have reflected Hosmer's transcendental leanings. From the back, the relaxation of the Faun's perfect muscles contrasts the animated textures of the tiger fur, stone pedestal, moss, and tree stump. Of the several versions of the sculpture, the size and the arrangement of the lion skin, the placement of grapes, and other sylvan accoutrement may change location or formation slightly, but the Faun always remains the same. Hosmer had success with her earlier full-size female figures: *Oeone* (1855), *Beatrice Cenci* (1856), *Tomb of Judith Falconnet* (1858), and *Zenobia* (1859). She also had great success with her fancy piece, *Puck* (1855). *The Sleeping Faun* was her first attempt at a life-size male. Here Hosmer counter balances the Faun's passive sensuality with the mischievous desexualized child/animal. By adding the impish satyr to the composition of the unsuspecting Faun, Hosmer accomplishes two things. She adds an element of humor that was rarely seen in the ancient sculptural precedents and she neutralized the otherwise overt sensuality, which may have been perceived to be beyond the limits of decorum for a woman of her time. That perception, in and of itself, could have diminished the chances for the work's critical and financial success.

Several art historians have speculated that the Faun bore a close resemblance to Hosmer. This makes it all the more interesting that a female sculptor, who never married, who only had romantic relationships with women and who was a prototype tomboy would have cast herself as the languidly sensual Faun.

1.Cornelia Carr (ed.), *Harriet Hosmer: Letters and Memories*. New York: Moffat, Yard and Company, 1912, p. 209.

Portrait of Wayman Crow
2007
watercolor on paper, 15 x 12 in.

Portrait of Wayman Crow, 1866
Two known versions
Marble • 25 x 14 3/4 x 10 3/4"
Signed and dated (verso): "Rome M.D.C.C.C.LXV – Tribute of Gratitude.
Harriet Hosmer Sculpt."
Two known versions, one marble, one plaster

Provenance

Collection
a. *Present Owners*
Washington University Gallery of Art, St. Louis, MO
Gift of the heirs of Wayman Crow, Sr., 1868
WU 2061
Previous Owners
Wayman Crow, Sr.
b. *Present Owners*
Plaster
Watertown Free Public Library, Watertown, MA
Gift of Mr. Lovell Thompson, 1974
Exhibitions
City Art Museum of St. Louis, St. Louis, MO, 1940, 1945, 1954
Washington University Gallery of Art, St. Louis, MO, 1961
Beginnings: The Taste of the Founders. Washington University Gallery of Art, St. Louis, MO, 2000
Collecting Patterns. Washington University Gallery of Art, St. Louis, MO, 2003
Harriet Goodhue Hosmer. Mildred Lane Kemper Museum, St. Louis, MO, 2008

Hosmer sculpted several portraits of her devoted male father figures and mentors: Dr. McDowell, Wayman Crow, and John Gibson. Hosmer was never romantically involved with men. But, her close personal and professional relationships with men reassured her public that she was at least being supervised by men.
Crow was a wealthy merchant turned state legislator, founder of Mercantile Library and Washington University in St. Louis. He also was the father of her best childhood friend and classmate, Cornelia Crow, who would edit *Harriet Hosmer: Letters and Memories*. To say that Wayman Crow was a father figure would be an understatement. His crucial support of Hosmer's career, financial assistance, management of her finances, and their constant written correspondence included a great deal of familial emotion and affection. He furthered her career, was instrumental in securing commissions, and was her loyalist patron. She nicknamed him "Pater." Hosmer was godmother to Wayman's granddaughter, Cornelia's daughter, who was named Harriet Hosmer Carr.

"One thing is past denial, that however successful I may become in my profession, it is to you that I owe all. The great thing in every profession, and most certainly so in art, is to get a good 'start,' as we Yankees say, and then all is right. When I look around and see other artists who have been here for years and still are waiting for a 'start' and then think what a friend I have in you, <u>sensa complimenti</u>, I wonder why I have been so much more blessed than my neighbors. Every successful artist in Rome, who is living, or who has ever lived, owes his success to <u>his</u> Mr. Crow."
Letter to Wayman Crow, October 12, 1854

References for this work must have been very important, especially because Wayman Crow did not sit for the portrait. In fact, it was a surprise gift for him from Hosmer. Art historians have suggested the bust of Perikles in the Vatican Museum Collection in Rome as a possible source of inspiration. The herm and bust portrait of Socrates in the Musei Capiltolini is also a sculpture Hosmer would have known. By quoting the herm and bust form from Antiquity, Hosmer elevates Wayman to the status of great men. Bare chested, a thick head of wavy hair, he appears virile and wise.

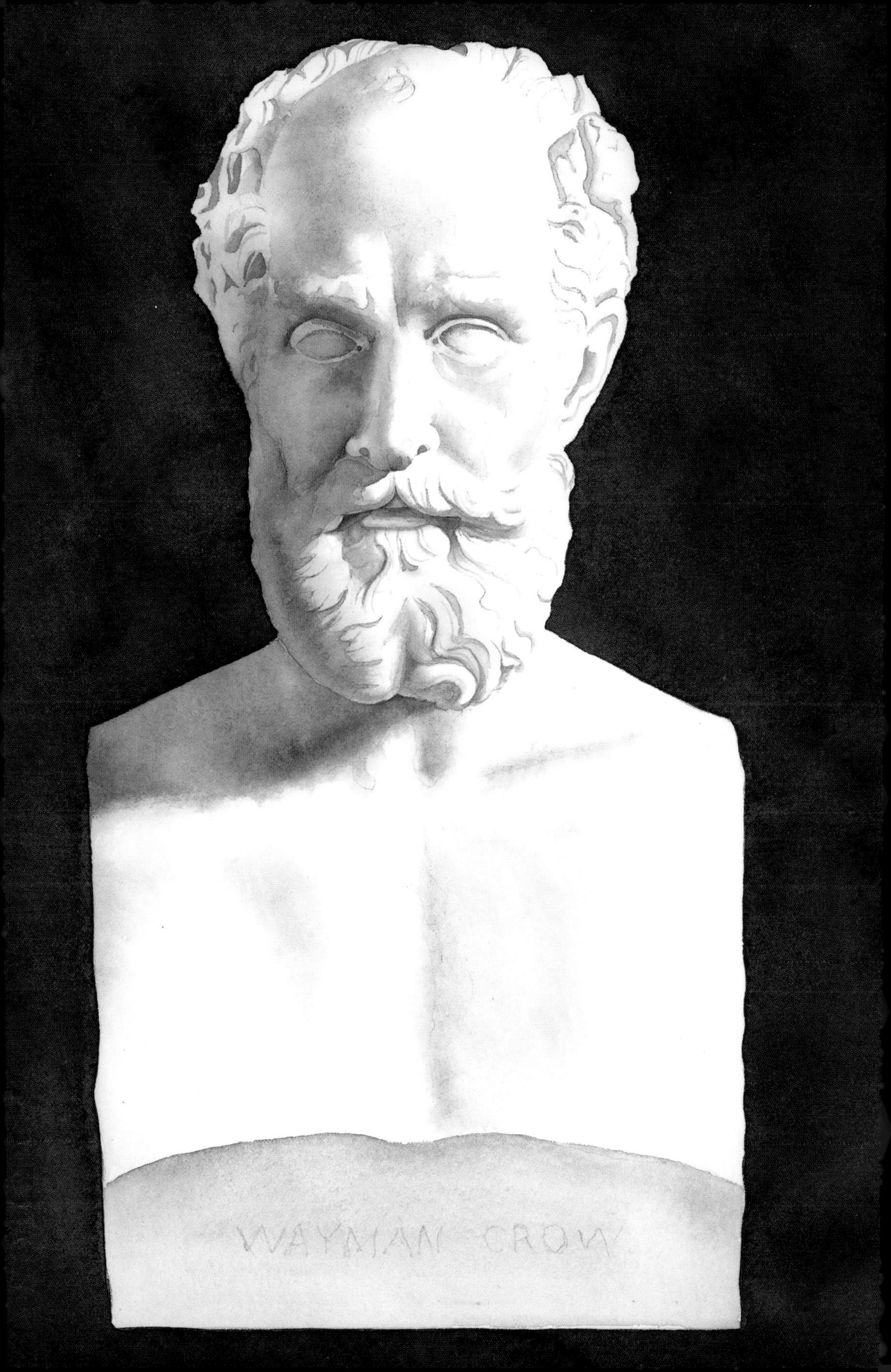
WAYMAN CROW

JOHN GIBSON
2007
watercolor on paper, 12 x 15 in.

John Gibson, 1866
Two known versions
Marble medallion • 11 1/2" diameter
Signed and dated (verso): "I. Gibson"

PROVENANCE

Collection
a. *Present Owners*
Watertown Free Public Library, Watertown, MA
Gift of Harriet Hosmer Carr, 1923
Previous Owners
Harriet Hosmer Carr
b. 13 1/8" diameter
Present Owners
National Portrait Gallery, London, England, 1980
NPG 5342
Previous Owners
Mr. R.G. Coats

John Gibson (1790–1866), the student of Thorvaldsen and Canova, was the most famous neo-classical sculptor living in Rome. Gibson was renowned for his "tinted" marbles, especially his *Tinted Venus*.

When twenty-two-year-old Harriet Hosmer arrived in Rome in 1852 and sent John Gibson two daguerotypes of her *Hesper* bust and her certificate in anatomy from the St. Louis Medical College, Gibson said, "Send the young lady to me, and whatever I know, and can teach her, she shall learn." Gibson had never had a student before and Hosmer would be his only one. Hosmer apprenticed with him for six years before she hung out her own shingle. As with any close student/teacher or artist/assistant relationship, he made many beneficial introductions for her and would be the male voice of authority to vouch for her artistic merit and virtuous character if needed. And it was.

The marble medallion is beautifully rendered. Bas-relief is extremely difficult to do because one has to sculpt an optical illusion in three dimensions. Bas-relief is the link between the illusion of reality in two dimensional painting and the reality of sculpting forms in the round.

Hosmer would have made her teacher proud, idealizing him as a young man. Gibson was sixty-one when they first met and seventy-five when he died. In this effigy, Hosmer depicts him as a youthful man with an elegant profile and pronounced cheekbones. The carving is subtle with the lightest touch. Soft wisps of hair curl and tuck in at the end.

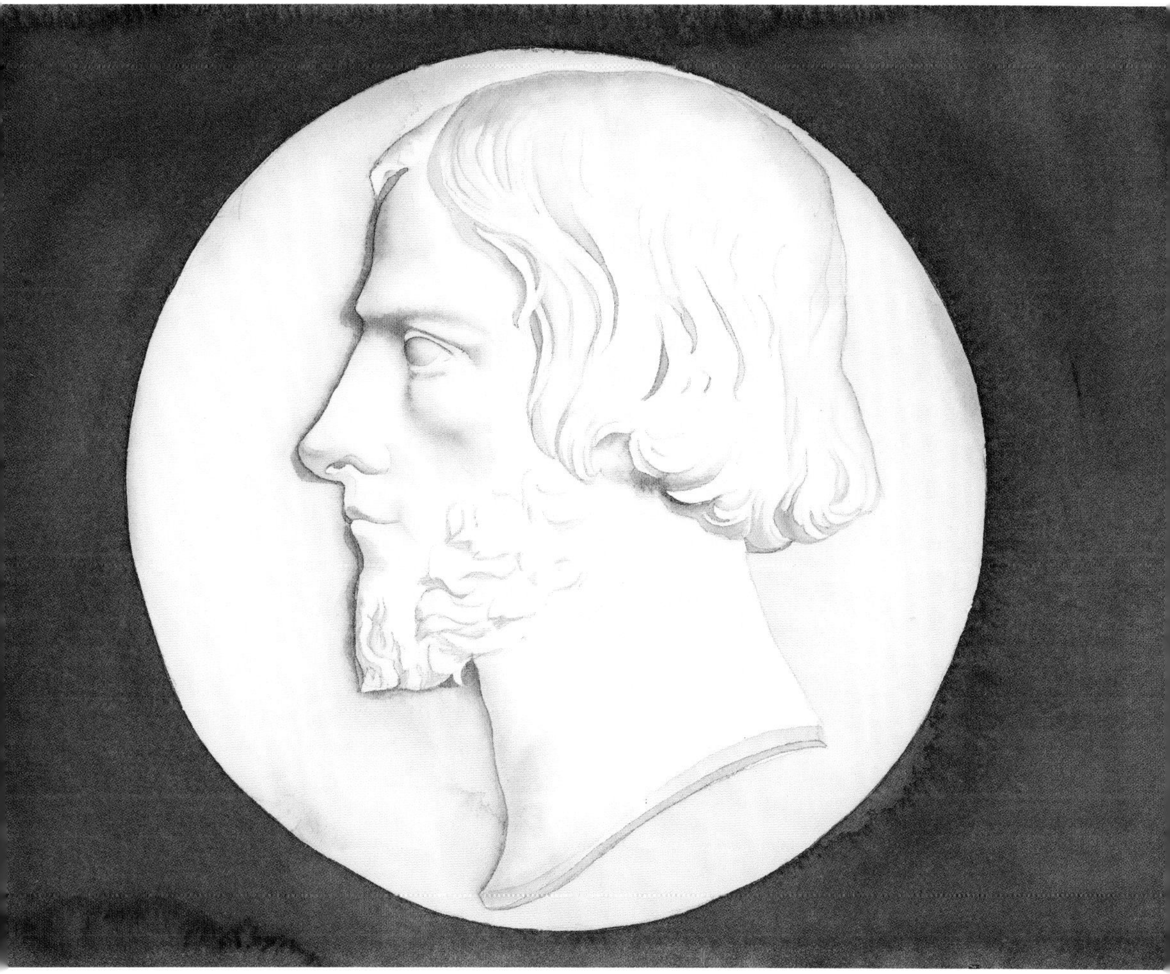

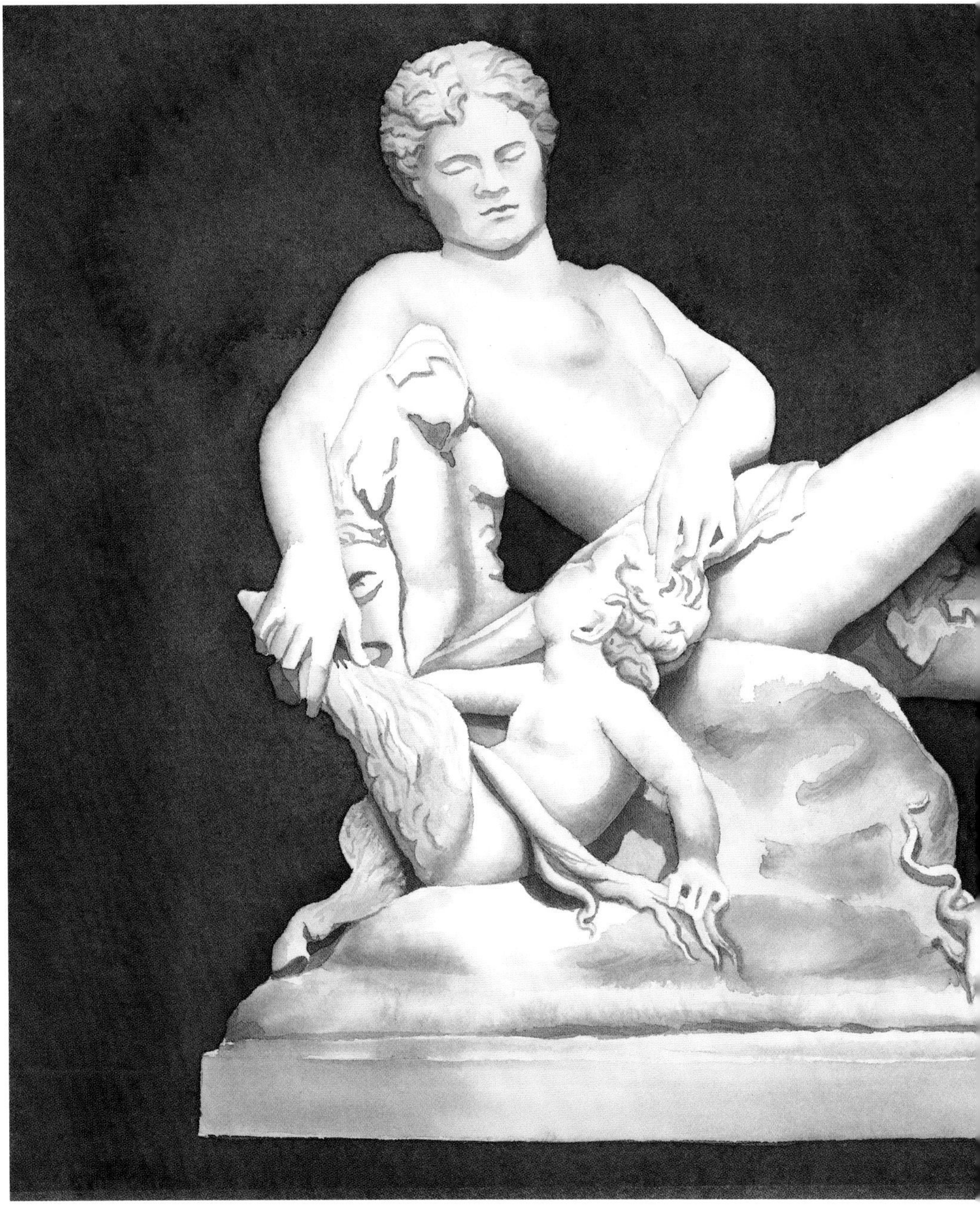

The Waking Faun
2007
watercolor on paper, 12 x 15 in.

The Waking Faun, 1866–1867
Marble or plaster • Life-size
Signed and dated (verso): unknown

Provenance

Collection
Present Owners
Unknown, thought to be destroyed

Hosmer created this as a companion to her very successful *The Sleeping Faun* (1865). It was intended for Lady Louisa Ashburton, her long time lover, who already owned *The Sleeping Faun*. But, it is unclear if it was ever realized in marble.

As was the practice, collectors would see a clay or plaster version of a sculpture in the artist's studio and place an order for the marble. Letters from Hosmer attesting to orders or hopes of the completed sculpture being included in future exhibitions don't guarantee that the work was, in fact, ever finished. It is also unclear if the existing photograph of *The Waking Faun* in Hosmer Collection in the Watertown Free Public Library is the version she destroyed, or the second one she wrote that she had started.

The Waking Faun is the mirror opposite of *The Sleeping Faun*. *The Waking Faun*'s right leg is crossed over the left, his feet are animated and pointed, and both his hands are now occupied with grasping the baby satyr as he sits up alertly. The baby satyr is now in front of the Faun, his prank having been discovered by the Faun.

This alertness might account for why it was considered more stylized and slightly stiffer.

Lincoln Memorial
2007
watercolor on paper, 12 x 15 in.

Lincoln Memorial, sometimes known as *Freedmen's Monument*, 1867–1868
Two known variations
Plaster • Height unknown
Signed and inscribed (verso): unknown

Provenance

Collection
Present Owners
Location unknown
Unknown, thought to be destroyed
Previous Owners
Unknown
Exhibitions
Boston, MA, 1868

Hosmer vigorously campaigned for three Lincoln Memorial competitions. The first was the *Lincoln Memorial* in Springfield, Illinois, the second was the *Freedmen's Monument* for the Capital building in Washington, D.C., and the third, was the *Crerar Lincoln Memorial* in Chicago, in 1889.
The *Lincoln Memorial* and the *Freedmen's Monument* were two almost identical submissions. Although Hosmer won neither, her designs were her most ambitious. It is a shame that all that remains of the plaster model are damaged, folded, faded photographs in the Watertown Free Public Library in Watertown, Massachusetts.
It is difficult to make out the specifics of the design. Written accounts describe a large square architectural footprint with multi-figure group installed around a raised domed "temple of fame" at the center of the design. Beneath this domed structure lay a recumbent Lincoln lying on a sarcophagus, with intricate bas-relief carving fit for a deceased Roman emperor and two different sets of freestanding figures. One group of four figures illustrates the historical progress of African Americans from slavery to courageous Union troops. The other set of figures, positioned at the furthest corners of the monument, appear to be angels with lowered trumpet, an honor guard for a fallen, martyred American hero.

In the second variation, the only difference is that all funerary references have been replaced by a standing Lincoln inside the "temple of fame," and the angels and African Americans have switched places.

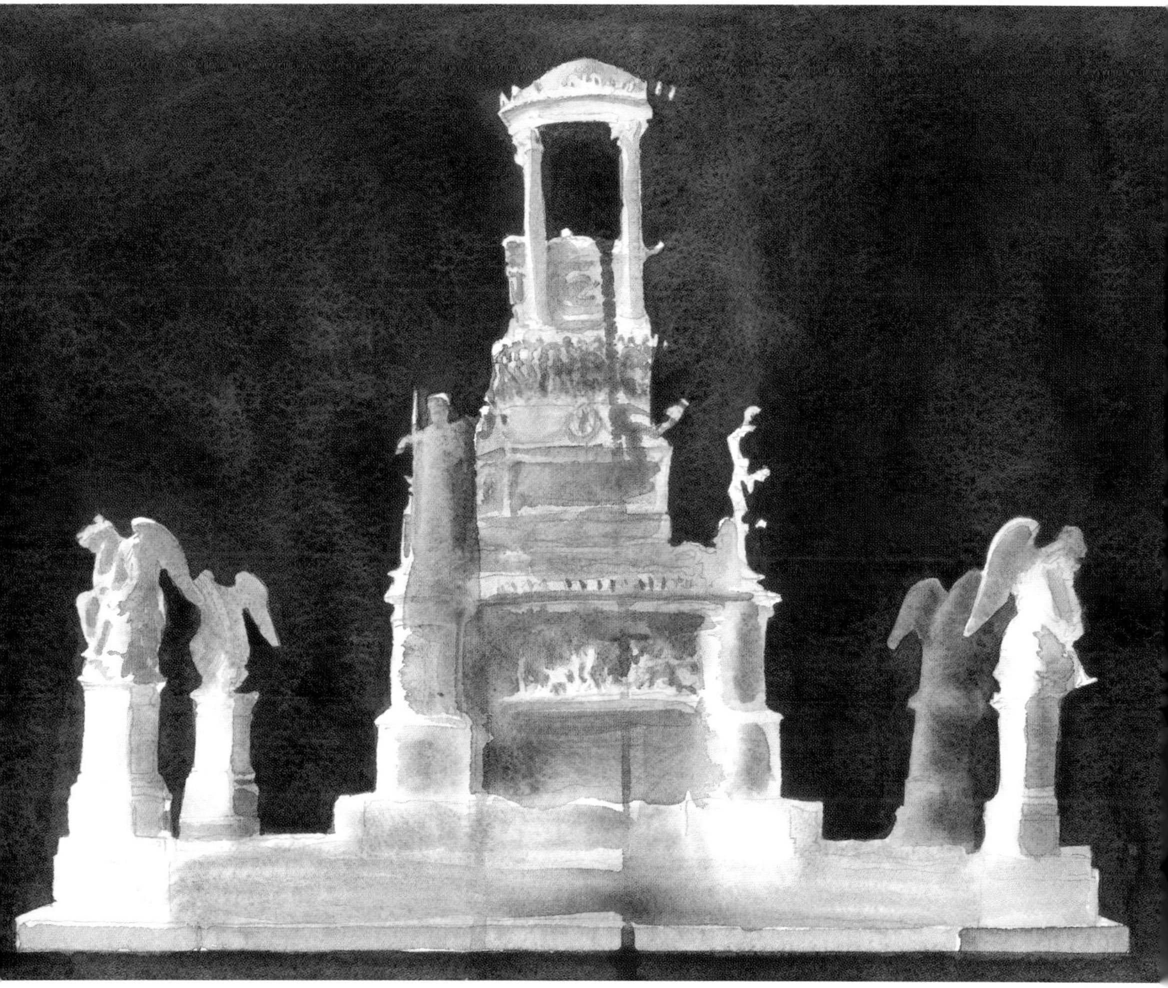

Queen of Naples

2007

watercolor on paper, 15 x 12 in.

Queen of Naples, 1868

Marble • Life-size

Provenance

Collection

Present Owners

Unknown

Signed and dated (verso): unknown

Inscribed (recto): "Gaetae Maria Regina"

Previous Owners

Unknown

The *Queen of Naples* is the second of the three full size statues of celebrated female sovereigns Hosmer chose to represent over the course of her career. Her first was *Zenobia, Queen of Palmyra* (1859), followed by the *Queen of Naples* (1868), and her final work, *Queen Isabella of Castile* (1891–1894).

The *Queen of Naples* is the only full-length portrait that Hosmer modeled from life. It is unclear if it was a commission or if it was ever purchased. Although *The Times* said "It will be considered her masterpiece," its location is unknown. No visual documentation of the statue survives, only numerous written accounts in newspapers, art magazines, and personal correspondence. Thus, there are conflicting reports about the work's progress and what it actually looked like. Whether it was ever translated into marble or only realized in clay remains a question. Did the Queen of Naples ever assume ownership of it? Hosmer was a personal friend of the Queen. Did Hosmer send it to her in Paris, where she lived in exile? It was seen in Hosmer's studio as late as 1872 and, although art historians have speculated that it returned to Germany with the Queen, its last known location was Castle Ashby, the home of the 7th Marquess of Northampton, Northamptonshire, England in 1891.

Maria Sophia (1841–1925), a Bavarian Bourbon princess, married Prince Francis II in 1859. When his father, King Ferdinand II, died, they ruled the Kingdom of Naples and the Two Sicilies for a brief but historic period. Garibaldi, on his campaign to unify Italy, invaded Naples in 1860. The King and Queen of Naples fled to Gaeta and it is here where she became famous for her acts of courage. Her husband, by all accounts, was a terrible leader. He had no military training, was insecure and indecisive. Instead, she led the troops at the siege of Gaeta (1860–1861) exhibiting great bravery. She instantly became a heroine to European royal women and developed a cult-like following. Garibaldi and Victor Emmanuel II were victorious. With the unification of Italy imminent, the Royal couple lived in exile in the Bourbon owned Palazzo Farnese in Rome with the permission of the Pope, ruler of the Papal States. It was during their stay in Rome that the Queen became friendly with Hosmer. But, in 1870, when Italian unification became official, they fled Italy forever.

According to the various descriptions written by visitors to her studio and detailed in the press and letters sent home from travelers on the Grand Tour, Hosmer created a life-size marble statue idealizing her most heroic moment on the battlegrounds of Gaeta. Hosmer posed the Queen in her costume of that time, a long billowing military cape enveloped her. She stood erect, her handsome head thrown back, a look of both disdain and resolution on her face. Her luxurious hair is braided and woven like a crown on her head. One hand was placed proudly on her breast as the cloak continued thrown over her shoulder. The other arm pointed downward to a pile of cannonballs at her feet that are adorned with modern riding boots reminiscent of ancient sandals. A pedestal takes on the appearance of a battleground. And the inscription on the pedestal reads "Gaetae Maria Regina."

Hosmer indicated her increasing interest in women's position in the world by portraying a real life heroine assuming a traditionally male role as a military hero. In fact, this costume of a draped cloak covering the figure is reminiscent of Hosmer's *Senator Benton* statue. One foot sported a Roman/modern boot hybrid, moved actively forward, stressed the willingness to be bold, and connected contemporary and ancient heroines.

It was common knowledge that Maria Sophia visited Hosmer's studio often to pose for the statue so that the likeness was perfect. It was also rumored they were romantically involved.

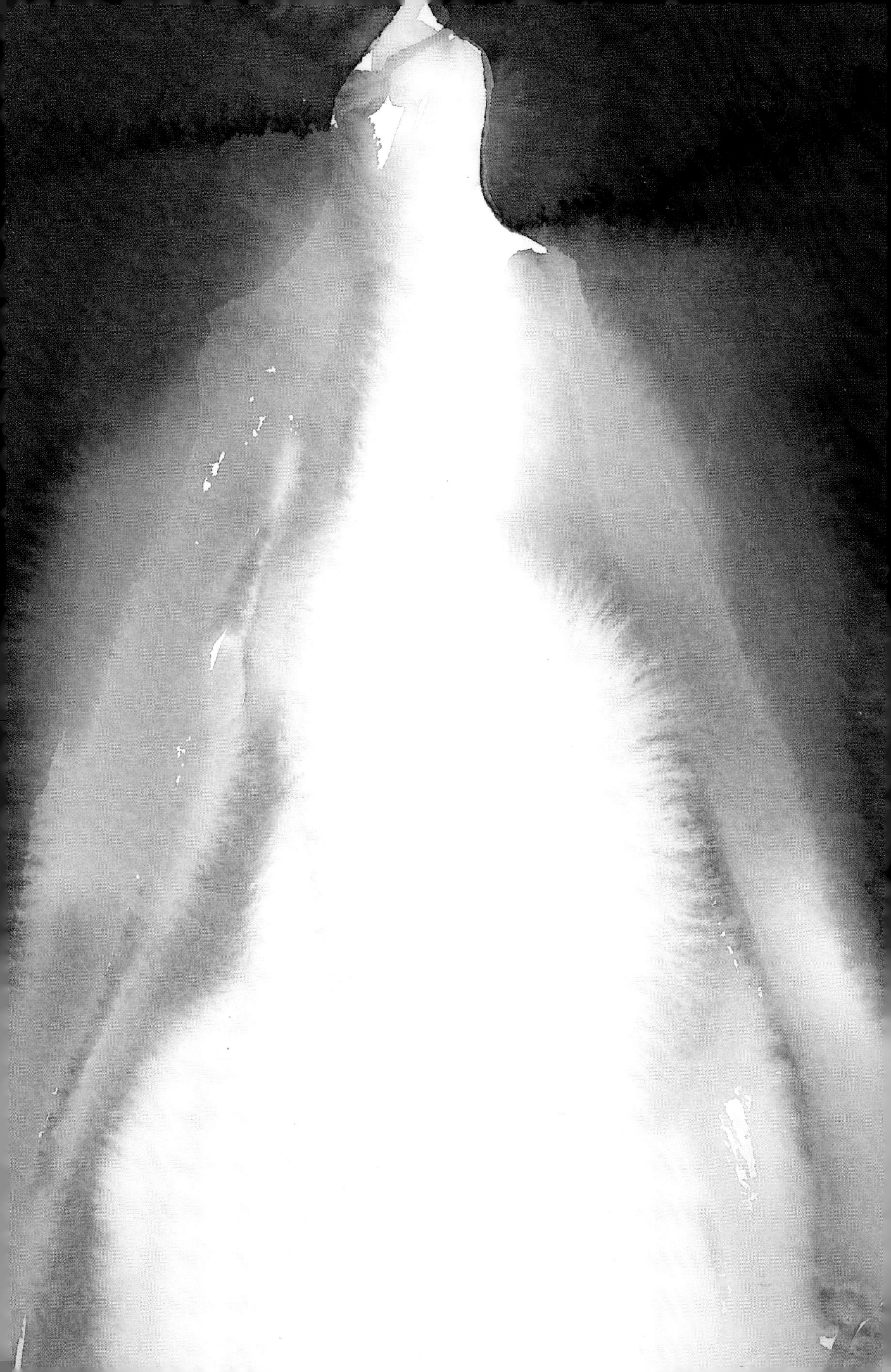

Sentinel of Pompeii

2007
watercolor on paper, 15 x 12 in.

Sentinel of Pompeii, 1878
Plaster and wax • Size: over 8'
Signed and inscribed (verso): unknown

Provenance

Collection
Present Owners
Location unknown
Previous Owners
Unknown
Exhibitions
Colnaghi's Gallery, Haymarket, London, 1878

Although there is a photograph of a damaged photograph of a photograph of a rough plaster bust of a ancient military male attributed to Hosmer in the Watertown Free Public Library, there is no way to confirm if it is definitely her Sentinel of Pompeii. It is especially uncertain because at the time, written accounts described Hosmer's new technique of modeling wax ever so smoothly over plaster casts.

The subject of Mount Vesuvius erupting and burying Pompeii in 79 CE fascinated writers and artists ever since it was discovered in 1748 and the excavation began. Popular nineteenth-century interpretations of the courageous or vulnerable in the face of devastation included Baron Edward Bulwer Lytton's *The Last Days of Pompeii* (1834) and Randolph Rogers's sculpture *Nydia, the Blind Flower Girl of Pompeii* (1855).

Hosmer chose to sculpt an actual figure with a moving story. A dutiful sentry, this Roman solider refused to flee imminent danger and became entombed, buried alive in the pumice and volcanic ash. His bones and armor were found at his guard post in 1794. His breast plate, helmet, and lance were moved to the Bourbon Museum in Naples where Hosmer studied them.

The London Times described the statue as:

"The figure is eight feet in height, clad in helmet and corselet of bronze plates modeled after the originals, leaning upon his lance in vain resistance to the deadening influence of the sulphurous fumes and the falling dust and ashes. His eyes are already closed. The blood in his veins thickens and runs slow. Looking at the figure in profile, we see that he already staggers and can scarce sustain himself by aid of his lance, hard clutched and pressed as a point of support against his knee. Besides his helmet and corselet he wears only a short tunic and sandals, showing the instep and toes, so that the limbs are freely displayed, and there is at once the least possible concealment of the figure and the least possible advantage derived from drapery.
The perfect simplicity and sincerity of the treatment give to Miss Hosmer's design the impressiveness which befits its subject."

The subject of ordinary people called to extreme acts of courage in the face of death resonated strongly with Hosmer throughout her career.

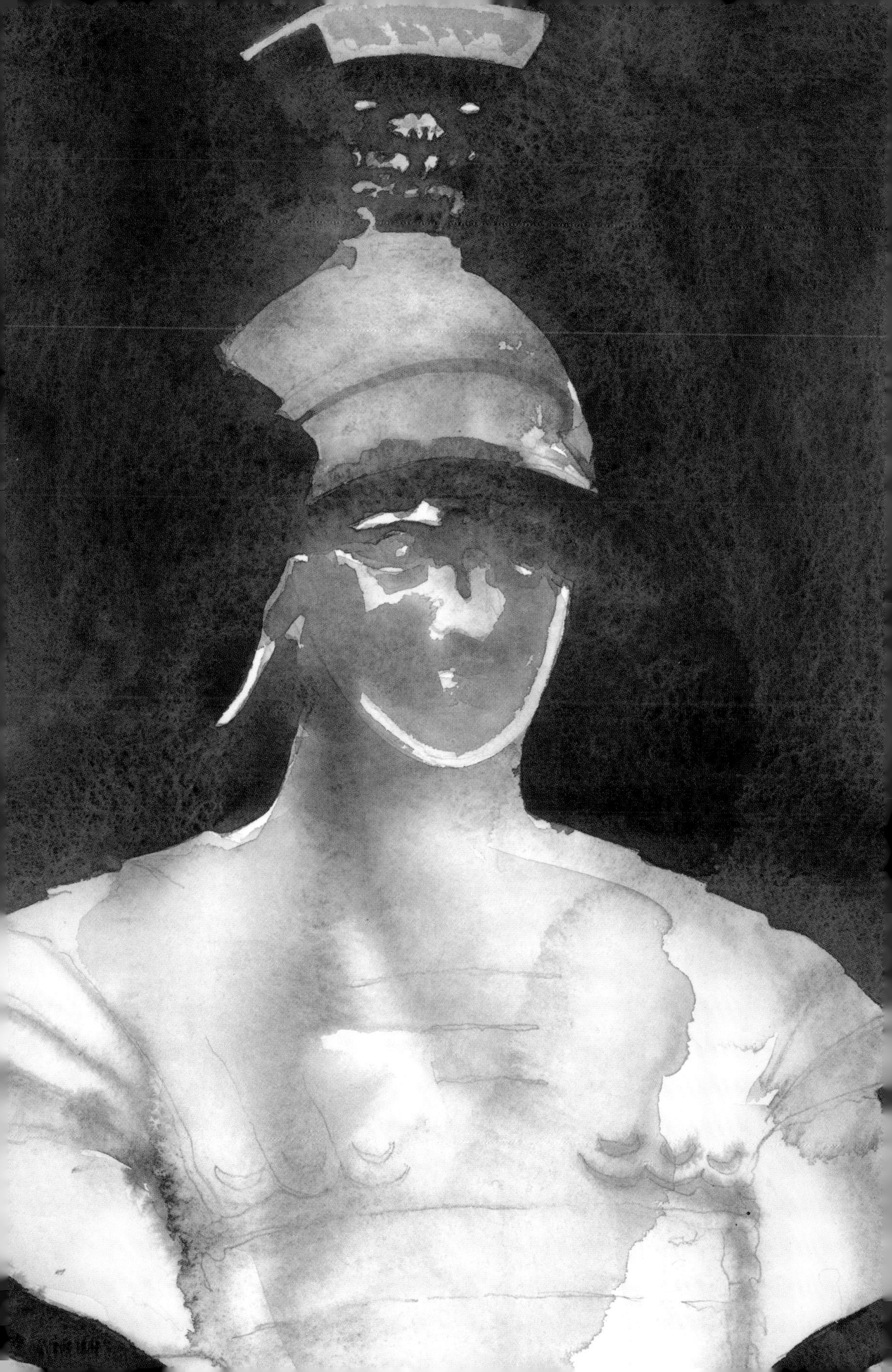

Crerar Lincoln Memorial -
The African Sibyl
2007
watercolor on paper, 15 x 12 in.

Crerar Lincoln Memorial - The African Sibyl,
1888–1896
Plaster and wax
Signed and inscribed (verso): unknown

Provenance

Collection
Present Owners
Unknown, probably destroyed

This is Hosmer's fourth and final attempt to win a Lincoln Memorial competition. Only a faded photograph of a sketch of one of the three figures in the design survives today at the Watertown Free Public Library.
Mr. John Crerar, a wealthy Chicago financier, left a bequest of $100,000 for a statue to be made of Abraham Lincoln. The competition was six years long and drawn out, due to a lawsuit against the estate filed by distant relatives. Several artists were invited to submit models and paid $2,500 to produce them. Hosmer exchanged numerous letters with the committee over the six years, explaining different problems she encountered creating, shipping, and delivering the model. It is unclear if they ever saw it.
Hosmer's three-figure design included a larger than life *Lincoln* above *The African Sibyl* and *Mourning Victory*. It is possible that *The African Sibyl* began as an independent design that was incorporated into her grander proposal for the Crerar Lincoln Memorial.
The African Sibyl portrayed a colossal ancient female prophet foretelling the future of her race to a young African male seated at her feet. She is looking up hopefully, we suppose, at Lincoln, holding a scroll that quotes him, "If slavery is not wrong nothing is wrong." Hosmer said if the Sibyl stood up, she would be over eleven feet high.
Mourning Victory is kneeling holding a lowered trumpet and wearing a laurel crown, the mood melancholic. This may have been a revised angelic figure from Hosmer's other Lincoln designs.
Hosmer wrote:

"This I consider the triumph of my desire to incorporate the classical beauty of outline and grace with a modern subject, in a manner that will, at a glance, tell its own story."

A photograph of the design was given to the Brownings, who showed it to Alfred Lord Tennyson, all of whom were sources of great inspiration for Hosmer. Tennyson is reported to have said: "It is the most poetic rendering in art, of a great historical truth, I have ever seen."
The commission eventually went to Augustus Saint Gaudens.

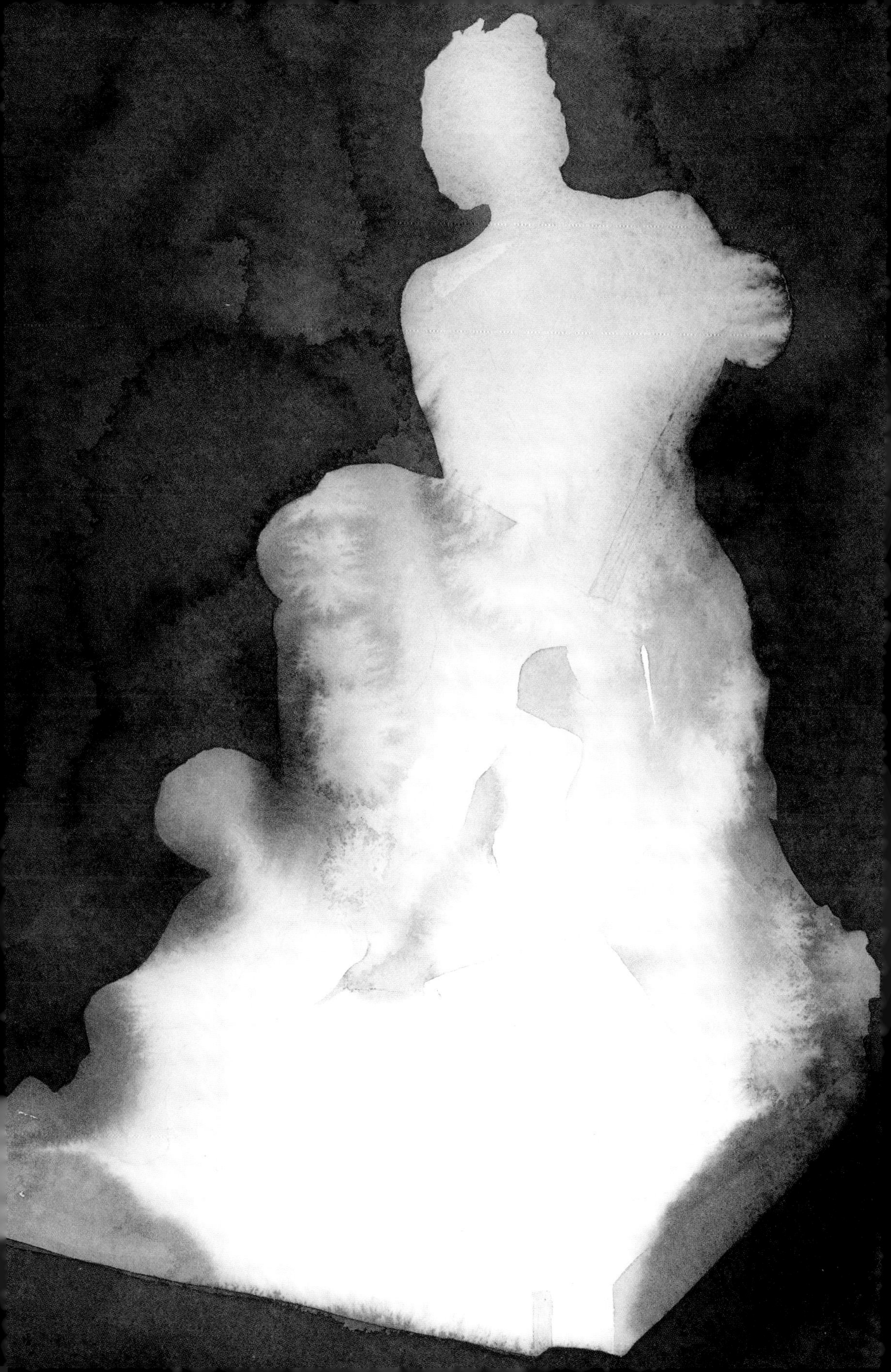

The Staghound
2007
watercolor on paper, 12 x 15 in.

The Staghound, Date unknown
Clay • Height unknown
Signed and inscribed (verso): unknown

Provenance

Collection
Present Owners
Unknown
Previous Owners
Empress of Austria

The Empress of Austria commissioned Hosmer to sculpt one of her favorite staghounds. She was the sister of Maria Sophia, the Queen of Naples, and part of the aristocratic circle of female friends, lovers, and collectors of Hosmer's works. Hosmer indicated in letters that she was also sculpting Caesar and his mate, two Saint Bernard dogs owned by Lady Ashburton. No descriptions or photographs remain. A photograph of *The Staghound* is in the Watertown Free Public Library.

Possible art historical references include the variety of Greek and Roman sculptures of dogs in the Vatican Museum Collection. Hosmer certainly would have known Horatio Greenough's marble *St. Bernard Dog* (1844) on the Perkins plot in Mount Auburn Cemetery in Cambridge, Massachusetts, just down the road from her childhood home.

Dog, man's and apparently woman's best friend, seems to have been a perfect subject for neo-classical sculptures. Horses and dogs were the stuff of royal life and were popular subjects for domestic commissions. Or were they portraits? These neo-classical dogs were always posed in their stereotypical role: alert, keeping guard, and protecting the hearth, the door, or the grave.

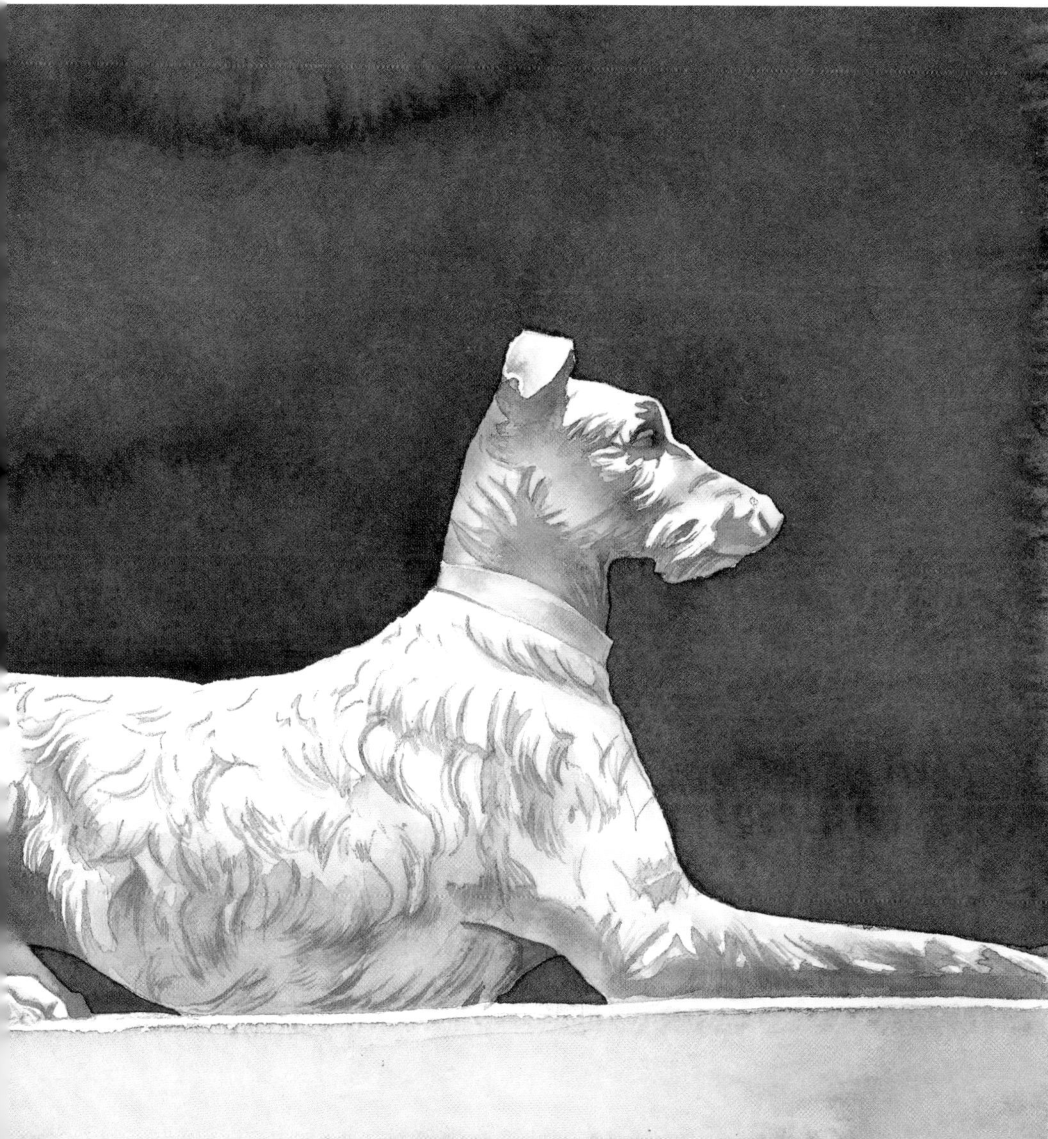

Dolphin Fountain
2007
watercolor on paper, 15 x 12 in.

Dolphin Fountain, Sometimes known as *Triton Fountain*, 1892
Marble • Height: unknown
Signed and inscribed (verso): unknown

Provenance

Collection
Present Owners
Unknown
Previous Owners
Lady Louisa Ashburton
Melchet Court, Hampshire, England

The Dolphin, sometimes known as *Triton Fountain*, was the male companion to Hosmer's *The Mermaid's Cradle*. The pair of marble fountains was commissioned by Lady Ashburton, Hosmer's long time lover, for her country house, Melchet Court, in Hampshire, England. They were installed in the Italian Gardens at Melchet Court, and *The New International Encyclopedia* reports both fountains there in 1903. In 1935 the estate was sold and the fountains were removed.
There are no written descriptions or photographs of the *Dolphin Fountain*.
Today, their whereabouts are unknown and Melchet Court is a Catholic school for boys with behavioral and emotional problems.

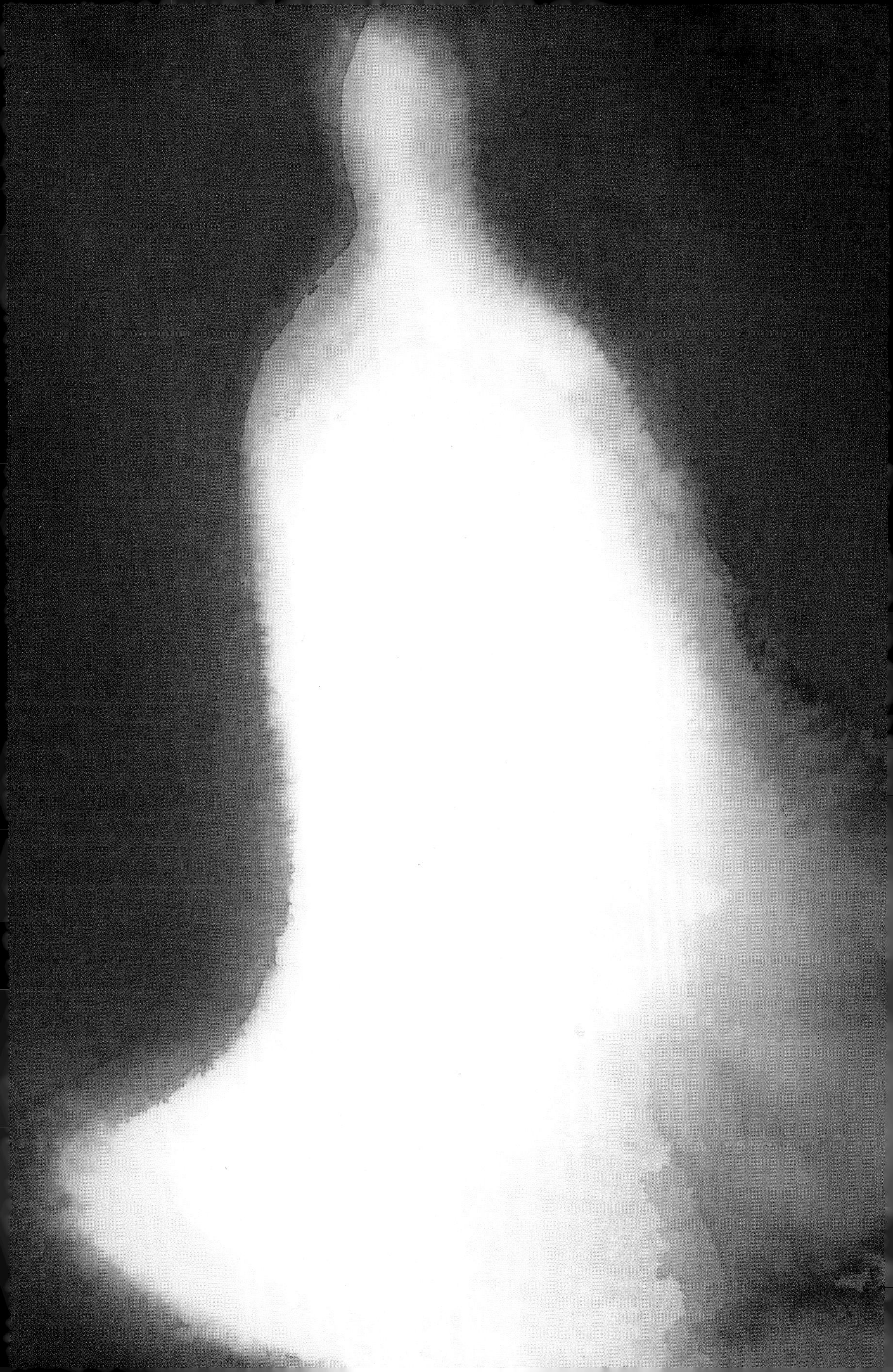

THE MERMAID'S CRADLE
2006
watercolor on paper, 15 x 12 in.

The Mermaid's Cradle, 1892–1893
Marble, Bronze • 7'
Signed and inscribed (verso):
Inscribed (recto): "THE MERMAID'S CRADLE"

Provenance

Collection
Present Owners
Fountain Square, Flint Park, Larchmont, NY
Gift of Helena Flint, in memory of her father, T.J.S. Flint, 1894 and donated the land for Flint Park, in 1915
Previous Owners
Helena Flint, Larchmont, NY
Previous Owners
Lady Louisa Ashburton, Melchet Court, Hampshire, England

The Mermaid's Cradle and *The Dolphin* were a female and male pair of marble fountains Lady Ashburton commissioned for her country house, Melchet Court, in Hampshire, England. They were installed in the Italian Gardens at Melchet Court, and *The New International Encyclopedia* reports both fountains there in 1903. Today, their whereabouts are unknown. However, the bronze version of the fountain is in Flint Park in Larchmont, NY.

The gigantic bronze mermaid is playing a reed pipe; her muscular torso is nude from the waist up. Waves of water crash around her hips as she straddles a rocky coast. Her scaled tales are long, slippery, and curl around a sleeping baby mermaid. The weight of the Mermaid's tail encircling the babe is convincing and the variety of textures are expertly sculpted.

Although the patina is damaged by weather and pollution, the form is intact and the fountain appears to work. *The Mermaid's Cradle* is Hosmer's only remaining complete fountain.

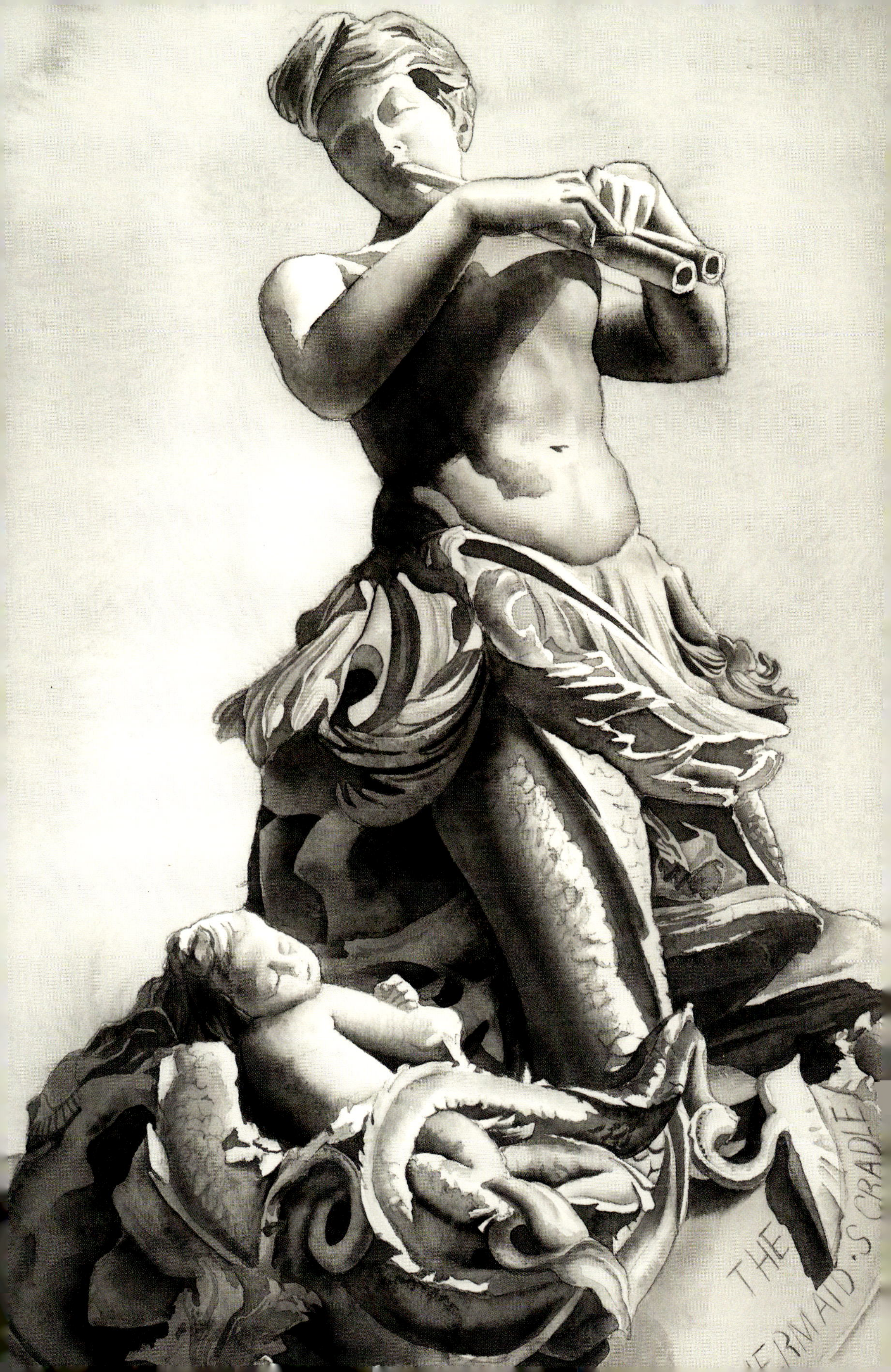
THE
ERMAID·S CRADLE

Queen Isabella of Castile
2007
watercolor on paper, 15 x 12 in.

Queen Isabella of Castile, 1893
Plaster [staff] • Larger than life-size
Signed and inscribed (verso): unknown
(base, recto): "________________ OWN CROWN OF CASTILE
_____ READY TO PLEDGE MY JEWELS
O MEET EXPENSES OF THE EXPEDITION"
(pedestal, recto): "QUEEN ISABELLA OF CASTILE GIVING HER JEWELS TO COLUMBUS"

Provenance

Collection
Present Owners
Unknown, thought to be destroyed
Exhibitions
World's Columbian Exposition. Chicago, IL, 1893
Mid-Winter's Fair. San Francisco, CA, 1894

Queen Isabella of Castile is the last known completed work by Hosmer and the last of her three celebrated female sovereigns. It was commissioned by the Daughters of Isabella, a Chicago based suffragist organization for the World's Columbian Exposition 1893. The Queen Isabella Society Suffragists sold one-dollar certificates to raise the funds for the sculpture. Hosmer, Anne Whitney, and other female sculptors refused to exhibit their work in the Women's building and exhibited in the Statuary Hall instead. The work was shown in the Mid-Winter fair in 1893 in San Francisco where it is believed to have been destroyed in the Great Earthquake of 1896.
There are indications that Hosmer corresponded with Pope Gregory IX, provided him with a drawing or two, and that he then bought a bronze of the statue. However, the Vatican Museum has no Hosmers in their collection nor any records of the correspondence. They suggested that Pope Gregory IX, as the King of the Papal States at the time, could have taken any objects that he bought while Pope with him when he retired.
Hosmer's design imagined Queen Isabella as a co-discoverer of the "New World." Stepping down from her throne, her arms reaching out, dripping in jewels and an abundance of folds of elaborate Orientalist drapery. She offers Columbus money in her left hand, and jewels in her right hand to fund his voyage to the "New World." Her right foot is actively stepping forward, much like *Zenobia*'s.
To Hosmer, Isabella seemed a perfect subject for the women's rights group. The sculpture was to be exhibited at an international world's exposition celebrating the anniversary of Columbus discovering America. But, the monumental statue was controversial. Some saw Isabella as a religious bigot who funded the Inquisition and a cruel leader who taxed her citizens heavily. Those that saw her as a compassionate visionary, pawning her jewels to finance Columbus expedition, thought that the criticism was fueled by anti-Catholic sentiments.
And thus, Hosmer went out with a bang, ending her artistic career with this majestic statue of a historically significant woman.

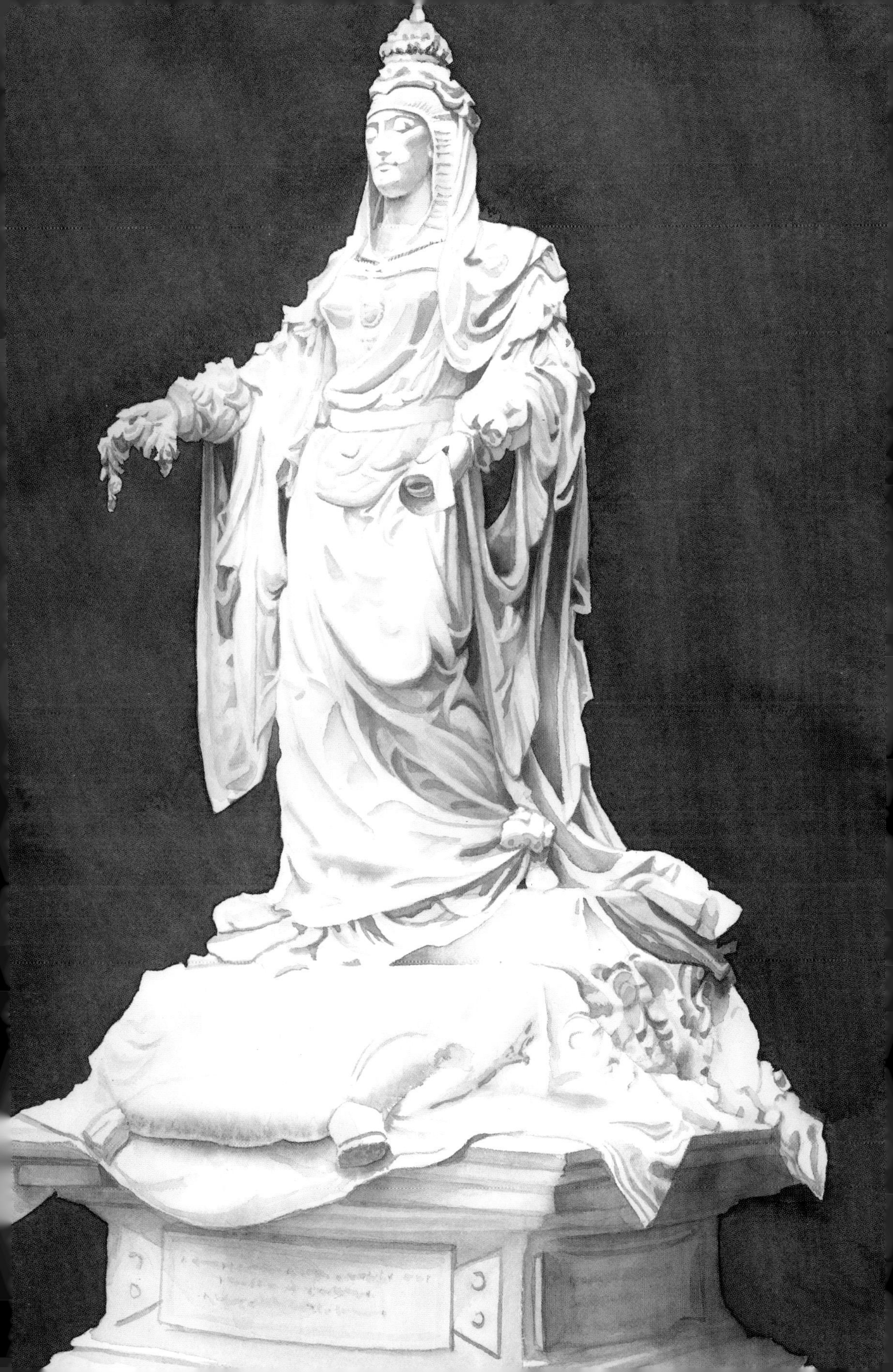

Appendix

Bibliography

Manuscript Collections

Ashburton Papers. Edinburgh, Scotland: National Library of Scotland.

Harriet Goodhue Hosmer. Watertown, MA: Watertown Free Public Library.

Harriet Goodhue Hosmer Papers. Cambridge, MA: Schlesinger Library, Radcliffe College, Harvard University.

Primary Texts

Armstrong, Tom. *200 Years of American Sculpture*. New York: Whitney Museum, 1976.

Carr, Cornelia (ed). *Harriet Hosmer: Letters and Memories*. New York: Moffat, Yard and Company, 1912.

Chadwick, Whitney. *Women, Art, and Society*. London: Thames & Hudson, 1990.

Cherry, Deborah. "Harriet Hosmer's *Zenobia*: A Question of Authority," in *Beyond the Frame: Feminism and Visual Culture, Britain 1850–1900*. London: Routledge, 2000, pp. 101–141.

Clark, Henry Nichols Blake and William H. Gerdts. *A Marble Quarry: The James H. Ricau Collection of American Sculpture at the Chrysler Museum of Art*. Manchester, VT: Hudson Hills Press, 1997.

Colbert, Charles. "Harriet Hosmer and Spiritualism," *American Art*, 10.3, 1996, p. 47.

Corrin, Lisa G. *Mining the Museum: An Installation by Fred Wilson*. Baltimore, The Contemporary and New York: The New Press, 1994.

Culkin, Katherine Louise. "'Slight a Girl as She Was': Gentility, Reform, and Harriet Hosmer." Unpublished Ph.D. Dissertation, Department of History, New York University, 2002.

Curran, Joseph L. *Hosmeriana: A Guide to Works by and about Harriet G. Hosmer*. Unpublished, 1975.

Dabakis, Melissa. "The Eccentric Life of a Perfectly 'Emancipated Female': Harriet Hosmer's Early Years in Rome," in Tolles, Thayer (ed.), *Perspectives on American Sculpture before 1925*. New York: Metropolitan Museum of Art, 2003, pp. 24–43.

Faxon, Alicia. "Images of Women in the Sculpture of Harriet Hosmer," *Women's Art Journal*, 2.1, 1981, pp. 25–29.

Fryd, Vivien Green. "The 'Ghosting' of Incest and Female Relations in Harriet Hosmer's Beatrice Cenci," *Art Bulletin*, 88, 2006, pp. 292–309.

Gerdts, William H. "The *Medusa* of Harriet Hosmer," *Bulletin of the Detroit Institute of Arts*, 56, 1978, pp. 96–107.

Gerdts, William H. *American Neo-Classical Sculpture: The Marble Resurrection*. New York: Viking Press, 1973.

Gopinath, Gabrielle. "Harriet Hosmer and the Feminine Sublime," *Oxford Art Journal*, 28.1, 2005, pp. 61–81.

Green, Shoshanna. "Harriet Hosmer: Sculpting Women and Men," *Gender & History*, 6.1, 1994, pp. 10–12.

Groseclose, Barbara S. "Harriet Hosmer's *Tomb to Judith Falconnet*: Death and the Maiden," *American Art Journal*, 12.2, 1980, pp. 78–89.

Hawthorne, Nathaniel. *The Marble Faun*. New York: Penguin Books, 1860.

Hawthorne, Nathaniel. *The Italian and French Notebooks*. Charleston, SC: BiblioBazaar, 2008.

James, Henry. *William Wetmore Story and Friends*. Boston: Houghton, Mifflin & Co., 1903.

Kasson, Joy S. *Marble Queens & Captives: Women in Nineteenth-Century American Sculpture*. New Haven and London: Yale University Press, 1990.

Kelly, Sarah E. "Zenobia, Queen of Palmyra," *Art Institute of Chicago Museum Studies*, 30.1, 2004, pp 8–9.

LaBarre, Margaret Wendell. "Harriet Hosmer: Her Era and Art," Unpublished Master Thesis, Department of Art History, University of Illinois, 1966.

Leach, Joseph. "Harriet Hosmer: Feminist in Bronze and Marble," *The Feminist Art Journal*, 5, 1976, pp. 9–13, 44–45.

Mariani, Andrea. "Sleeping and Waking Fauns: Harriet Goodhue Hosmer's Experience of Italy, 1852–1870," in Jaffe, Irma B. (ed.), *The Italian Presence in American Art 1760–1860*. New York: Fordham University Press, 1989, pp. 195–207.

Markus, Julia. *Across An Untried Sea: Discovering Lives Hidden in the Shadow of Convention and Time*. New York: Knopf, 2000.

McCarthy, Katherine Margaret. "Harriet Hosmer's *Beatrice Cenci*: Male Domination and Dangerous Females," Unpublished Graduate Thesis for MA in Art History, University of Virginia, 1994.

Parker, Rozika and Griselda Pollock. *Old Mistresses: Women, Art and Ideology*. New York: Pantheon Books, 1981.

Parrott, Sara Foose. "Expatriates and Professionals: The Careers in Italy of Nineteenth-century American Women Writers and Artists," Unpublished Ph,D. Dissertation, The George Washington University, 1988.

Rensselaer, Susan. *Antiques*, 84.4, 1963, pp. 425–426.

Sherwood, Dolly. *Harriet Hosmer, American Sculptor, 1830–1908*. Columbia: University of Missouri Press, 1991.

Stebbins, Thomas E. *The Lure of Italy, American Artists and The Italian Experience 1760–1914*. Boston: Museum of Fine Arts and New York: Harry N. Abrams, Inc., 1992.

Tolles, Thayer. *American Sculpture in The Metropolitan Museum of Art. Volume 1: A Catalogue of Works by Artists Born before 1865*. New York: The Metropolitan Museum of Art, New York, 1999.

Van Rensselaer, Susan. "Harriet Hosmer," *Antiques*, 84.1, 1963, pp. 424–428.

Vicinus, Martha. "Laocooning in Rome: Harriet Hosmer and Romantic Friendship," *Women's Writing*, 10.2, 2003, pp. 353–366.

Waller, Susan. "The Artist, the Writer, and the Queen: Hosmer, Jameson, and Zenobia," *Woman's Art Journal*, 4.1, 1983, pp. 21–29.

Withers, Josephine. "Artistic Women and Women Artists," *Art Journal*, 35.4, 1976, pp. 330–336.

Zastoupil, Carol. "Creativity, Inspiration, and Scandal: Harriet Hosmer and Zenobia," in Jaffe, Irma B. (ed.), *The Italian Presence in American Art 1760–1860*. New York: Fordham University Press, 1989, pp. 195–207.

Select Secondary Texts

"Affairs in Rome," *New York Evening Post*, January 5, 1865, p. 1.

American Art in The Newark Museum, 1981, p. 244.

American Art Journal, 5, pp. 21–66.

"American Artists in Europe," *New York Evening Post*, June 21, 1866, p. 1.
"American Female Sculptors," *Frank Leslie's Illustrated Newspaper*, 22.563, 1866, p. 259.
"American Genre Painters: Eastman Johnson, Winslow Homer and the Rest," *The New York Times*, August 25, 1875, p. 10.
"American Lady Sculptors," *Daily Alta California*, September 17.
"American Paintings, Drawings and Sculpture," *Sotheby's*, May 22, 1996.
"American Women Artists," *Dwight's Journal of Music*, 13.25, 1857, p. 173.
Antiques, 122, 1982, p. 1154.
"An Artist in Rome: Miss Hosmer Entertains a Large Audience at Grace Methodist Episcopal Church," *The Daily News* [Denver, Colorado].
Art Association of Indianapolis, Indiana: A Record 1883–1906. Published on the Occasion of the John Herron Art Institute November 20, 1906. Indianapolis: The Hollenbeck Press, 1906, pp. 10–11.
"Art Gossip," *Cosmopolitan Art Journal*, 2:38.
Art in America, May–June 1971, p. 67.
"Art in Continental States," *The Art Journal*, 1868, p. 256.
"Art in Continental States: Rome," *The Art Journal*, 25, 1873, p. 12.
The Art Interchange, 31.3, 1894, p. 80.
The Art Journal, 1867, pp. 218–219.
The Art Journal, March 1, 1868.
The Art Journal, May 1872.
Art Journal Illustrated Catalogue of the International Exhibition of 1862. London: James S Virtue, 1862.
"Art Matters," *Boston Evening Transcript*, May 24, 1866, p. 2.
"Art Matters," *Boston Transcript*, January 14, 1857, p. 1.
"Art Musings," *The Art Journal*, 1.10, 1868, p. 133.
"Baylor University's Browning Collection and Other Browning Interests," *The Baylor Bulletin*, 30.4, 1927.
"The Beatrice Cenci," *The Crayon*, 4.12, 1857, p. 379.
Boston Museum of Fine Arts. Proceedings at the Opening of the Museum of Fine Arts with the Reports for 1876. Boston: Alfred Mudge & Sons, 1876.
Browingiana in Paylor University. Waco, TX: Baylor University, 1921.
Bulletin of the City Art Museum of St. Louis, 12, 1927, pp. 50–52.
Catalogue of the A.T. Stewart Collection of Paintings, Sculpture, and Other Objects of Art. New York: J.J. Little and Co., 1887.
Catalogue of Modern & Renaissance Sculpture. St. Louis: City Art Museum, 48, 1920.
Catalogue of the Works of Art in the St. Louis Mercantile Library.
The Commonwealth, 3.18, 1864, p. 3.
"Correspondence," *The Art Journal*, 26, 1864, p. 27.
Cosmopolitan Art Journal, November 1856, p. 90.
Cosmopolitan Art Journal, March 1858, p. 142.
The Crayon, 1857, p. 379.
The Crayon, 1857, p. 150.
Dia Bulletin, 55.1, 1976, p. 8.
Dia Bulletin, 56.2, pp. 96–107.
Dwight's Journal of Music, 1.22, 1852, pp. 171–172.
Dwight's Journal of Music, 24.24, 1865, p. 396.
"Farewell to Miss Hosmer," *San Francisco Chronicle*, March 31, 1894.
"The Fine Arts," *The Independent*, 6.316, 1854, p. 401.
"The Fine Arts at Dublin International Exhibition of 1865," *The Month*, 3, 1865, pp. 186–193.
"Foreign Art Notes," *New York Evening Post*, May 24, 1872, p. 1.
"The Freeman's Monument to Abraham Lincoln," *The Art Journal*, 7, 1868, p. 6.
"Glimpses of the Fair," *The Chicago Evening Journal*, June 14, 1983.
A Guide to the Works of Art in the St. Louis Mercantile Library. St. Louis, MO: Missouri Democrat Book and Job Printing House, 1871.
A Guide to the Sculpture, Paintings, and Other Objects of Art, in the Halls of the St. Louis Mercantile Library Association. St. Louis, Mo: George Knapp & Co., 1859.
A Guide to the Sculpture, Paintings, Coins and other Objects of Art in the Halls of the St. Louis Mercantile Library Association. St. Louis, MO: Missouri Democrat Book and Job Office, 1862.
Harper's Weekly, 4.187, 1860, p. 467.
Harper's Weekly, June 20, 1868, pp. 396–398.
"Harriet Goodhue Hosmer (1830–1908)," *Gateway Heritage*, 3.4, 1983, pp. 16–18.
"Harriet Hosmer," *Boatswain's Whistle* [Boston], November 18, 1864.
"Harriet Hosmer," *The Bookman*, 65, 1913, p. 114.
"Harriet Hosmer," *Brooklyn Daily Eagle*, April 2, 1893, p. 4.
"Harriet Hosmer," *Cosmopolitan Art Journal*, 3, 1859, pp. 214–217.
"Harriet Hosmer," *Dwight's Journal of Music*, 13, 1858, pp. 195–196.
"Harriet Hosmer," *Dwight's Journal of Music*, 17.21, 1860.
"Harriet Hosmer-Charlotte Chushman," *Colman's Rural World and Valley Farmer*, 21, 1868, p. 108.
"Harriet Hosmer's Studio and the Model for the Lincoln Statue," *The Daily Inter Ocean*, June 14, 1890.
"In Honor of Miss Hosmer," *San Francisco Chronicle*.
"Hosmer, Harriet," *Boston and Boston People in 1850*. Farmington Hills, MI: Thomson Gale, 2005.
"International Exhibition 1862," *The Art Journal*, 1, 1862, pp. 113–116.
"The Isabella Idea," *Washington Evening Star*, February 28, 1891.
"Italy," *Times* [London], May 24, 1872.
"Italy: From Our Own Correspondent," *The Times*, May 24, 1872, p. 10.
"John Gibson, R.A.," *The Art Journal*, 28, 1866, pp. 113–115.
"Lady-Artists in Rome," *The Art Journal*, 28, 1866, pp. 177–178.
"Lafayette Park," *The Central Magazine*, II.5.
"Letter from Rome," *The Art Journal*, 1.8, 1868.
"Letter from Rome," *The Art Journal*, 3.1, 1870.
"Letter from Rome," *The Art Journal*, 9, 1870, pp. 141–142.
"Letter From Rome," *The New Century For Woman, Exposition Volume, Philadelphia Centennial Exposition*. May 13–November 11, 1876, p. 47.
"The Life of Gibson, The Sculpture," *The Nation X*, 1870, pp. 273–274.

"The Life of Harriet Hosmer," *The Nation*, 95, 1912, pp. 340–342.
"The Life and Works of Harriet Hosmer," *New England Magazine*, November 1911.
Lines of a Different Character, American Art from 1727 to 1947. New York: Hirschl & Adler Galleries, 1982.
A Marvelous Repose: American Neo-Classical Sculpture, 1825–1876. New York: Hirschl & Adler Galleries, 1997, pp. 20–21.
"Minor Topics: The 'Pompeian Sentinel,' by Miss Hosmer," *The Art Journal*, 10, 1878, p. 189.
"Miss Harriet Hosmer, The American Sculptor," *Ballou's Pictorial*, December 5, 1857.
"Miss Hosmer's Beatrice Cenci," *Dwight's Journal of Music*, 12.4, 1857, pp. 236–237.
"Miss Hosmer's Beatrice Cenci," *The New York Times*, November 12, 1857, p. 4.
"Miss Hosmer's Oenone," *New York Evening Post*, March 30, 1857, p. 2.
"Miss Hosmer's 'Pompeian Sentinel,'" *The Arc*, 1878, p. 56.
"Miss Hosmer's Plans," *Chicago Herald*, May 16, 1890, p. 9.
"Miss Hosmer's Progress," *Dwight's Journal of Music*, 9.1, 1853, p. 7.
"Miss Hosmer's Statue of Zenobia," *New Path*, 2, 1865, p. 53.
"Miss Hosmer's Studio at Rome," *Harper's Weekly*, May 7, 1859, pp. 293–294.
"Miss Hosmer's Zenobia," *New York Evening Post*, November 12, 1864, p. 2.
"'Most Famous of American Women Sculptors' Miss Harriet Hosmer of Watertown," *The Boston Globe*, March 1, 1908.
The Nation, February 27, 1908, p. 203.
"National Academy of Design," *New York Daily Tribune*, May 20, 1865, p. 6.
The New York Times, March 10, 1879, p. 5.
The New York Times, July 16, 1879, p. 4.
New York Tribune, 1852.
"A New Work of Art: Harriet Hosmer's Masterpiece – A Monument to Abraham Lincoln," *New York Evening Post*, December 13, 1866, p. 1.
"Obituary: Mr. Alfred Gately," *The Art Journal*, 25, 1863, p. 181.
"Our Survey of Literature, Science, and Art," *The Cornhill Magazine*, 6, 1862, pp. 153–156.
"Our Weekly Chat," *The Jewish Progress*, December 1893.
"Our Weekly Gossip," *The Athenaeum*, December 19, 1863, p. 840.
"Personal," *Home Journal*, May 12, 1860, p. 2.
"Personal Items," *Boston Transcript*, May 28, 1859, p. 2.
"Puck," *The Art Journal*, 14, 1875, p. 312.
"Puck Engraved by G. Stodart from the Sculpture by Miss Hosmer," *The Art Journal*, May 1875, p. 317.
Putnam's Monthly, 5.26, 1855, p. 224.
"Queen Isabella and Her Latest Detractor," *The Monitor*, 38.43, 1894.
"Queen Isabella: Miss Hosmer's Statue of the Spanish Ruler May Remain Here," *San Francisco Chronicle*.
"The Rabbi and The Queen," *San Francisco Chronicle*.
"Recollections of the Brownings," *The Youth Companion*, 74, 1900, pp. 599–600.
"Reviews and Literary Notices: Art Thoughts," *Atlantic Monthly*, 25, 1870, pp. 252–256.
"Reviews and Literary Notices: Book of the Artists," *Atlantic Monthly*, 25, 1868, pp. 255–256.
"Reviews and Literary Notices: Life of Gibson," *Atlantic Monthly*, 25, 1870, p. 126.
"Roman Studios," *The New York Times*, May 17, 1873, p. 7.
Scientific American, 81.8, 1899, p. 123.
"Sculpture," *Watson's Weekly Art Journal*, p. 69.
"Sculpture in America," *Harper's New Monthly Magazine*, 58, 1879, pp. 657–672.
"Sculpture: The Dublin Exhibition of 1865," *Temple Bar*, 15, 1865, pp. 15–19.
"A Sibyl," *The Art Journal*, 17, 1866, p. 54.
"Sketchings. Domestic Art Gossip," *The Crayon*, 2, 1857.
"Sketchings. Domestic Art Gossip," *The Crayon*, 7, 1860, p. 142.
"The Sleeping Faun," *The Art Journal*, 17, 1878, p. 220.
St. Louis Globe-Democrat [St. Louis, MO], December 13, 1888.
"The Studios of Rome," *The Art Journal*, 9, 1870, pp. 77–78.
"The Study of Art in Boston," *Harper's New Monthly Magazine*, 58, 1879, p. 58.
"Taste as South Kenington," *Temple Bar*, 5, 1862, pp. 470–480.
"Toleration in Art," *San Francisco Bulletin*, March 17, 1894.
Travelers in Arcadia: American Artists in Italy 1830–1897. Detroit: The Detroit Institute of Arts, 1951.
"Two Club Receptions: Miss Harriet Hosmer Entertained by the Century Ladies," *San Francisco Chronicle*.
"Unveiling of Benton's Statue," *The Missouri Republic*, May 24, 1868.
"Visits to the Studios of Rome," *The Art Journal*, June 1, 1871, p. 162–164.
"A Walk Through the Studios of Rome," *Art Journal*, 1854, pp. 350–354.
"Water Colorer," *The Crayon*, p. 56.
"What Women Are Doing," *Demorest's Family Magazine*, May 28, 1892.
"Women Artists," *The Living Age*, 817, 1860, pp. 245–248.
"Women Artists," *The Southern Review*, 5, 1869, pp. 299–322.
"The Women Artists of New York and Its Vicinity," *New York Evening Post*, February 24, 1868, p. 2.
"The Women Artists in ALL Ages and Countries," *Littell's Living Ag*, 64, 1860, p. 248.
"The Women Inventors," *Scientific American*, 81, 1899, p. 123.
"The Year at Sotheby Parke Bernet, 1976–77," *Art at Auction London: Sotheby Parke Bernet*, 1977.

Allen, Harriet Trowbridge. *"Sculptors' Studios." Travels in Europe and the East*. New Haven: Tuttle, Morehouse & Taylor, 1879.
Allen, Henry Watkins. "Letter No. XXX, Hotel d'Angleterre, Rome, Italy," in *The Travels of a Sugar Planter; Or, Six Months in Europe*. New York: J.F. Trow, 1861.
Backhman, Donna G. and Sherry Piland. *Women Artists: An Historical Contemporary and Feminist Bibliography*. N.J. and London: The Scarecrow Press: Metuchen, 1978.
Backstrom, Jane. "A Marmorean Flock," *The World*, 8. 1, 1994, pp. 28–30.
Barter, Judith A. *American Arts at The Art Institute of*

Chicago: From Colonial Times to World War I. Chicago: Art Institute of Chicago, 1998.

Beal, Graham. *American Beauty: Paintings and Sculpture From the Detroit Institute of Arts.* London: Scala, 2002.

Benjamin, Samuel G.W. "Sculpture in America," *Harper's New Monthly Magazine*, 58, 1879, p. 668.

Benton, Fremont Jessie. *Souvenirs of My Time.* Boston: d. Lothrop and Co., 1887.

Bjelajac, David. *American Art.* London: Laurence King Publishing LTD, 2004.

Bolas, Gerald. *"One Hundred Years of the Washington University Art Collection," illustrated Checklist - Of the Collection Paintings, Sculpture and Works on Paper.* St. Louis, Missouri: Washington University Gallery of Art, 1981.

Bolton, Sarah Knowles. *Lives of Girls Who Became Famous.* New York: T.Y. Crowell & Co., 1914.

Bradford, Ruth, A. "The Life and Works of Harriet Hosmer," *New England Magazine*, 45.2, 1911, pp. 265–269.

Brockhoff, Dorothy. "Harriet Hosmer Nineteenth-century Free Spirit," *Washington University Magazine*, 47.1, 1976, pp. 37–39.

Brooks, Van Wyck. *The Dream of Arcadia: American Writers and Artists in Italy 1760–1915.* New York: E.P. Dutton, 1958.

Busch, Jason T. Christopher Monkhouse, and Janet L. Whitmore. *Currents of Change: Art and Life Along the Mississippi River 1850–1861.* Minneapolis, MN: Minneapolis Institute of Arts, 2004.

Californian. "Queen Isabella and Harriet Hosmer," *Overland Monthly*, 23.134, 1894, pp. 222–223.

Chiarmonte, Paula. *Women Artists in the United States: A Selective Bibliography and Resource Guide On the Fine and Decorative Arts, 1750–1986.* Boston: G.K. Hall & Co., 1990.

Child, L. Maria. "Miss Hosmer's Zenobia," *Dwight's Journal of Music*, 1859, p. 228.

Child, L. Maria. "Miss Harriet Hosmer," *Littell's Living Age*, 20, 1858, pp. 697–698.

Clark, Nichols B. *A Marble Quarry: The James H. Ricau Collection of Sculpture at the Chrysler Museum of Art.* New York: Hudson Hills Press, Inc., 1997.

Clark, Nichols B. "Pairs of Sculptures Collected by James Ricau," *The Magazine Antiques*, November 1997, pp. 700–705.

Clement and Hutton. "Letter," *N.Y. Evening Post*, November 1878.

Clement, Clara Erskine. *Women in the Fine Arts, from the Seventh Century B.C. to the Twentieth Century A.D.* Charleston: Biblio Bazaar, 2007.

Cobbe, Frances Power. "Ireland and Her Exhibition in 1865," *Fraser's Magazine*, 72, 1865, pp. 403–422.

Cobbe, Frances Power. *Italics: Brief Notes on Politics, People, and Places in Italy in 1864.* London: Trubner and Co., 1864.

Cobbe, Frances Power. "What Shall We Do With Our Old Maids?," *Fraser's Magazine*, 66.145, 1862, pp. 594–611.

Cole, Jeremy. *Harriet Goodhue Hosmer, and Joseph Leo Curran. The Story of Harriet Hosmer.* 1999. VHS.

Conner, Janis. *American Sculpture: 1845–1925.* New York: Conner-Rosenkranz, 2001.

Cook, Cl. *National Academy of Design Reviews*, May 20, 1865.

Cooper, Emmanuel. *The Sexual Perspective: Homosexuality and Art in the Last 100 Years in the West, Second Edition.* London and New York: Routledge Press, 1994.

Craven, Wayne. *Sculpture in America.* New York: Thomas Y. Crowell Co., 1968.

Curran, Joseph L. *Watertown's Victorian Legacy: A Bicentennial Art Exhibition.* Watertown, MA: Watertown Public Library, 1976.

Cushing, Stanley Ellis and David B. Dearinger. *Acquired Tastes: 200 Years of Collecting for the Boston Athenaeum.* Boston, MA: Boston Athenaeum, 2007.

Dearinger, David B. (ed.). *Rave Reviews: American Art and Its Critics, 1826–1925.* New York: National Academy of Design, 2000.

Dearinger, David B. (ed.). "When Journalists Became Critics: The Birth of American Art Criticism," *Nineteenth Century*, 22.1, 2002, pp. 9–18.

Dickinson, Dr. Frances. *Queen Isabella Journal*, 1.4, 1890.

Eastlake, Lady Gibson Biography, 1870.

Edselas, F.M. "A Golden Age and Its People," *Catholic World Magazine*, February 1896.

Ellet, Mrs. E.F. *Women Artists in All Ages and Countries.* London: Richard Bentley, 1859.

Evans, Mark (ed.). *Princes as Patrons: The Art Collections of the Princes of Wales From the Renaissance to the Present Day, An Exhibition from the Royal Collection.* London: Merrell Holberton, 1998.

Fairbanks, Jonathan L. and Rebecca Ann Gay Reynolds. "The Art of Forest Hills Cemetery (Roxbury, Massachusetts)," *Magazine Antiques*, November 1 1998, pp. 696–703.

Faxon, Alicia and Sylvia Moore. *Pilgrims & Pioneers: New England Women in the Arts.* New York: Midmarch Arts Press, New York, 1987.

Florentina. "Walks Through the Studios of Rome," *The Art Journal*, 1854.

Fort, Ilene. *The Figure in American Sculpture: A Question on Modernity.* Baltimore: University of Washington Press, 1995.

Free, Renée. "European," *Art Gallery of New South Wales Handbook.* Davie, Annabel (ed.), 1988, pp. 36–56.

Fuller, Hiram. *Sparks from a Locomotive; Or, Life and Liberty in Europe.* New York: Derby & Jackson, 1859.

Gage, Matilda Joslyn. "Woman as Inventor," *The North American Review*, 136, 1883, pp. 478–489.

Gerdts, William H. "American Sculpture: The Collection of James H. Ricau," *Antiques*, 86, 1964, pp. 291–298.

Gerdts, William H. (ed.). *The White Marmorean Flock: Nineteenth-century American Women Neoclassical Sculptors.* Poughkeepsie, NY: Vassar College Art Gallery, 1972.

Gessi, Leone. *Rome.* Rome: La Libreria dello Stato, 1949.

Goldin, Marco. *American storie di pittura del nuovo mondo.* Treviso: Linea d'ombra libri, 2007.

Greenthal, Kathryn, Paula M. Kozol, and Jan Seidler Ramirez. *American Figurative Sculpture in the Museum of Fine Arts, Boston.* Boston: Museum of Fine Arts, Boston, 1986.

Greenwood, Grace. *Haps and Mishaps of a Tour in Europe.* Boston: Ticknor, Reed & Fields, 1854.

Groseclose, Barbara. "The Incest Motif in Shelley's The Cenci," *Comparative Drama*, 19, 1985, p. 224.

Harding, Jonathan. *The Boston Athenaeum Collection: Pre-Twentieth Century American and European Painting and Sculpture*. Boston, MA: Boston Athenaeum, 1984.
Harris, Ann Sutherland and Linda Nochlin. *Women Artists: 1550–1979*. New York: Alfred A. Knopf, 1976.
Hawley, Henry H. "Hosmer's Marble Faun," *Cleveland Art*, December 1997, pp. 4–6.
Hawthorne, Sophia. *Notes in England and Italy*. New York: G.P. Putnam & Son, 1869.
Heller, Nancy G. *Women Artists: An Illustrated History*. New York: Abbeville Press, 1987.
Helmuth, William Tod, (ed.). *Arts in St. Louis*. St. Louis: [s.n.], 1864.
Hirshler, Erica E. *A Studio of Her Own: Women Artists in Boston 1870–1940*. Boston: Museum of Fine Arts, Boston, 2001.
Hodges, Maud de Leigh. *Crossroads on the Charles: A History of Watertown. Massachusetts*. Carraan, NH: Phoenix Publishing, 1980.
Holmes, William H. *Catalogue of Collections, of the Smithsonian Institution, The National Gallery of Art*. Washington, D.C.: Government Printing Office, 1926.
Hoffman, Andrea. *Harriet Hosmer's Life and Work*. Unpublished Ph.D. dissertation, University of Southern California, 1979.
Hopkins, James Herron. "Letter," *Pittsburgh Post*, 1870.
Hosking, William J. "Lincoln's Tomb, Designs Submitted and Final Selection," *Journal of the Illinois State Historical Society*, 50, 1957, pp. 51–61.
Hosmer, George Leonard. *Hosmer Genealogy: Descendants of James Hosmer Who Emigrated to America in 1635 and Settled in Concord, Mass*. Cambridge, MA: Technical Composition Company, 1928.
Hosmer, Harriet. "Correspondence: Miss Hosmer's *Zenobia*," *The Art Journal*, January 1, 1864, p. 27.
Hosmer, Harriet. *The Crayon*, September 1860, p. 264.
Hosmer, Harriet. "Miss Hosmer's Letter in Vindication of American Sculptors," *Boston Daily Advertiser*, July 24, 1874, p. 2.
Hosmer, Harriet. "The Process of Sculpture," *Atlantic Monthly*, 14, 1864, pp. 734–737.
Howat, John K. and John Wilmerding. *19th-Century America: Paintings and Sculpture*. New York: The Metropolitan Museum of Art, 1970.
Howe, Julia Ward. *From the Oak to the Olive*, 1868.
Hoyle, Pamela and Jonathan Harding. *A Climate for Art*. Boston, MA: Boston Athenaeum, 1980.
Hyde, William, and Howard L Conrad. "Wayman Crow," *Encyclopedia of the History of St. Louis*, 1899.
Jaffe, Irma B. (ed.). *The Italian American Art, 1760–1860*. New York and Rome: Fordham University Press, 1989.
James, Bruce. "Western Collection: Paintings and Sculpture," *Art Gallery of New South Wales Handbook*, 1999, pp. 17–77.
Jarves, J. Jackson. "Progress of American Sculpture in Europe," *The Art Journal*, 33, 1871, pp. 6–8.
Karcher, Carolyn L. *The First Woman in the Republic: A Cultural Biography of Lydia Maria Child*. Durham: Duke University Press, 1994.
Kelly, Sarah E. "Zenobia, Queen of Palmyra," *Art Institute of Chicago Museum Studies*, 30.1, 2004, pp. 8–9.
Krichbaum, Jorg and Rein A. Zondergeld. *Kunstlerinnen: Von der Antike bis zur Gegenwart*. Koin, Germany: DuMount Buchverlag, 1979.
Leach, Joseph. *Bright Particular Star: The Life and Times of Charlotte Cushman*. New Haven and London: Yale University Press, 1970.
Leach, Joseph. "Harriet Hosmer: Feminist in Bronze and Marble," *The Feminist Art Journal*, 5, 1976, pp. 9–13, 44–45.
Lewis, Scott (ed.). *The Letters of Elizabeth Barrett Browning to Her Sister Arabella*. Waco, TX: Wedgestone Press, 2002.
Ludlow, Fitz-Hugh. "Art: Harriet Hosmer's *Zenobia*," *Atlantic Monthly*, February 15, 1865, pp. 248–250.
Luedtke, Luther S. *Nathaniel Hawthorne and Romance of the Orient*. Bloomington and Indianapolis: Indiana University Press, 1989.
MacAdam, Barbara J. *American Art at Dartmouth: Highlights from the Hood Museum of Art*. Hanover: Trustees of Dartmouth College, 2007.
MacAdam, Barbara J. "Building on Dartmouth's Historic American Collections: Hood Museum of Art Acquisitions since 1985," *The Magazine Antiques*, November 2007, p. 148.
MacAdam, Barbara J. *Marks of Distinction, Two Hundred Years of American Drawings and Watercolors from the Hood Museum of Art*. Manchester, VT: Hudson Hills Press, 2005.
MacAdam, Barbara J. "Hosmer's Medusa Acquired by Hood Museum," *VOX*, 15.10, 1996, p. 2.
Matthew, Rev. Gibson *Biographies*.
McCarthy, Kathleen D. *Women's Culture: American Philanthropy and Art, 1830–1930*. Chicago: The University of Chicago Press, 1991.
Miller, Florence Ferwick. "Art in the Woman's Section of the Chicago Exposition," *The Art Journal*, 40.13, 1883, pp. 13–16.
Nelson, Charmaine, A. *The Color of Stone: Sculpting the Black Female Subject in Nineteenth-century America*. Minneapolis and London: University of Minnesota Press, 2007.
Nochlin, Linda and Maura Reilly. *Global Feminisms*. New York: Perseus Distribuation Services, 2007.
Oldcastle, John. "An American Millionaire's Gallery," *The Art Journal*, 50, 1887, pp. 153–156.
Ormond, Richard. *Early Victorian Portraits*. 1973.
Park, Frank. "American Authors and Artists in Rome," *Lippincott's Magazine*, 8, 1884, pp. 491–495.
Parrott, Sara Foose. "Networking in Italy: Charlotte Cushman and 'The White Marmorean Flock,'" *Women's Studies*, 14, 1988, pp. 305–338.
Payne, Elizabeth Rogers. "Anne Whitney, Sculpture," *The Art Quarterly*, 25, 1962, pp. 244–261.
Peake, Elizabeth. *Pen Pictures of Europe*. Philadelphia: J.B. Lippencoll & Co., 1874.
Pentland, J.B. *A Handbook of Rome and Its Environs*. London: John Murray, 1873.
Petersen, Karen, and J.J. Wilson. *Women Artists: Recognition and Reappraisal from the Early Middle Ages to the Twentieth Century*. New York: Harper Colophon Books, 1976.
Piland, Sherry. *Women Artists: An Historical, Contemporary*

and Feminist Bibliography. Lanham, MD: The Scarecrow Press, Inc., 1994.
Prieto, Laura R. *At Home in the Studio: the Professionalization of Women Artists in America*. Cambridge, MA and London: Harvard University Press, 2001.
Ramirez, Jan Seidler. *Harriet Goodhue Hosmer*. Boston: Museum of Fine Arts, Boston, 1986.
Randall, Frank. *History of the Development of Building Construction in Chicago*. Urbana, IL: University of Illinois Press, 1949.
Randall, Lillian M.C. "An American Abroad: Visits to the Sculptors' Studios in the 1860s," *Journal of the Walters Art Gallery*, 33.34, 1971, pp. 48–49.
Remer, Abby. *Pioneering Spirits: The Lives and Times of Remarkable Women Artists in Western History*. Worcester, MA: Davis, 1997.
Reynolds, Gary A. *American Bronze Sculpture: 1850 to the Present*. Newark, NJ: The Newark Museum, 1984.
Roberson, Samuel A. and William H. Gerdts. "The Greek Slave," *The Museum*, 17, 1965, pp. 1–32.
Roos, Jane Mayo. "Another Look at Henry James and the 'White Marmorean Flock,'" *Woman's Art Journal*, 4, 1983, p. 32.
Rosenblum, Robert and H.W. Janson. *19th-century Art*. Upper Saddle River, NJ: Prentice Hall, 2004.
Rowlands, Walter. "Art Sales in America," *The Art Journal*, 50, 1887, pp. 293–295.
Rubinstein, Charlotte Streifer. *American Women Artists: From Early Indian Times to the Present*. Boston: G.K. Hall & Co., 1982.
Savage, Kirk. "'Freedom's Memorial': Manumission and Black Masculinity in a Monument to Lincoln," in Reynolds J. Scott-Childress (ed.), *Race and the Production of Modern American Nationalism*. New York: Garland Publishing, Inc., 1999, pp. 21–42.
Schluester, Dr. Robert E. "Joseph Nash McDowell's Medical (1805–1868), Sculptor," *Washington University Medical Alumni Quarterly*, 1, 1937, pp. 4–14.
Sherwood, Dolly. "My Dearest Mr. Crow," *Washington University Magazine*, 51.3, 1981, p. 7.
Slatkin, Wendy. *Voices of Women Artists*. Upper Saddle River, NJ: Prentice Hall, 1992.
Slatkin, Wendy. *Women Artists in History: From Antiquity to the 20th Century*. Engelwood Cliffs, NJ: Prentice Hall, 1985.
Stokstad, Marilyn. *Art: A Brief History. Second Edition*. Upper Saddle River, NJ: Prentice Hall, 2004.
Starr, Eliza Allen. "*Queen Isabella* Statue," *Queen Isabella Association*, May 1892.
Stebbins, Theodore E. Jr. *The Lure of Italy: American Artists and the Italian Experience*. New York: Harry N Abrams Inc., 1992.
Swanson, Peggy. "Author Compiling Stories of Statues and Paintings," *St. Louis Post-Dispatch*, February 7, 1965, pp. 2, 8–9.
Taft, Lorado. *The History of American Sculpture*. New York: The MacMillan Company, 1925.
Tarbell, Ida M. "Women as Inventors," *The Chautauquan*, 7, 1887, pp. 355–357.
Taylor, Sarah Wingate. "Harriet and The Browning Hands," *Yankee*, 21, 1957, pp. 44–47.
Terry, Robert J. "Recalling a Famous Pupil of McDowell's Medical College Harriet Goodhue Hosmer, Sculptor," *Washington University Medical Alumni Quarterly*, 7.2, 1944, pp. 59–65.
Thorp, Margaret Farrand. "Harriet Hosmer, Leader of 'The White Marmorean Flock,'" *Smith Alumnae Quarterly*, 1965, pp. 148–151.
Thorp, Margaret Farrand. *The Literary Sculptors*. Durham, NC: Duke University Press, 1965.
Thorp, Margaret Farrand, "The White Marmorean Flock," *New England Quarterly*, 32, 1959, pp. 147–169.
Thurston, Rev. R.B. "Harriet G. Hosmer," in James Parton (ed.), *Eminent Women of the Age*. Ann Arbor, MI: University of Michigan, 2005, pp. 566–598.
Tschudi, Clara. *Maria Sophia Queen of Naples*. New York: E.P. Dutton & Co., 1905.
Tufts, Eleanor, Gail Levin, Alexandra Comini, and Wanda M. Corn. *American Women Artists 1830–1930, The National Museum of Women in the Arts*. Washington, D.C.: International Exhibitions Foundation, 1987.
Walker, Katherine. "American Studios in Rome and Florence," *Harper's New Monthly Magazine*, 33, 1866, pp. 101–105.
Whiting, Lilian. *Italy: The Magic Land*. Boston: Little, Brown, and Co., 1910.
Van Ravenswaay, Charles. "Lafayette Park," *Bulletin of the Missouri Historical Society*, 14, 1958.
Vance, William L. *America's Rome*. New Haven and London: Yale University Press, 1989.
Vogel, Charity Ann. *American Virgins: Images of Virginal and Celibate Women in Nineteenth-century Literature and Art*. Unpublished Ph.D. Dissertation, Department of English, State University of New York at Buffalo, 2004.
Wallace, Elizabeth. "American Woman's Friendships," *Outlook*, 102, 1912, pp. 545–548.
Weil, Mark S. "The Serra Sculpture: How Public is a Public Monument?," *Saint Louis Literary Supplement*, 1.5, 1977.
Weimann, Jeanne Madeline. *The Fair Women: the Story of the Woman's Building, World's Columbian Exposition Chicago 1893*. Chicago: Academy Chicago Publications, 1987.
Wilmerding, John, Linda Ayers, and Earl A. Powell. *An American Perspective: Nineteenth-century Art from the Collection of Jo Ann and Julian Ganz Jr.* Washington, D.C.: National Gallery of Art, 1981.
Willard, Frances Elizabeth and Mary A. *A Woman of the Century*. Buffalo: Charles Wells Moulton, 1893.
Witzling, Mara R. *Voicing Our Visions: Writing by Woman Artists*. New York: Universe, 1991.
Wreford, Henry. "Lady-Artists In Rome," *The Art Journal*, 28, 1866, pp. 177–178.
Yellin, Jean Fagan. *Women and Sisters: The Anti-Slavery Feminists in American Culture*. New Haven and London: Yale University Press, 1989.

Patricia Cronin
(b. 1963 Beverly, MA)

Patricia Cronin's paintings, sculptures, and installations have been exhibited extensively in the United States and Europe, including solo exhibitions at the Brooklyn Museum, Deitch Projects and Brent Sikkema, New York, the American Academy in Rome Art Gallery, Rome, UB Art Gallery, University of Buffalo, NY, and group exhibitions at the Neuberger Museum, Purchase, NY, Aldrich Museum, Ridgefield, CT, Yale University Art Gallery, New Haven, CT, David Zwirner, New York, Alessandra Bonomo, and MACRO, Rome, Galleria Biagiotti Progetti Arte, Florence, Gallery of Modern Art, Glasgow, and COBRA Museum, Amsterdam.

Cronin is the recipient of numerous awards and grants including the Rome Prize, American Academy in Rome, the Louis Comfort Tiffany Foundation Award, the New York Foundation for the Arts Artist Grant, the Grand Arts Artist Grant, the Deutsche Bank Fellowship, the Pollock-Krasner Foundation Grant, and the Civitella Ranieri Foundation Fellowship.

She is an Associate Professor of Art at Brooklyn College of The City University of New York. She lives and works in New York.

William H. Gerdts

William H. Gerdts is a Professor Emeritus of Art History at the Graduate School of the City University of New York. He received his Bachelor of Arts degree from Amherst College and his Master's and Ph.D. degrees from Harvard University. Dr. Gerdts has been a curator at The Norfolk Museum, the Newark Museum, and Gallery Director at the University of Maryland. He was co-founder and Senior Lecturer in the Sotheby's American Art Institute for twenty years.

He is the author of over twenty-five books including *American Neoclassic Sculpture: The Marble Resurrection*, *The Great American Nude*, *Masters of the Humble Truth: Masterpieces of American Still Life, 1801–1930*, *American Impressionism*, *The New Path: Ruskin and the American Pre-Raphaelites* (with Linda Ferber), and *Monet's Giverny: An Impressionist Colony*.

Maura Reilly

Maura Reilly is an independent curator and writer. As the founding curator of the Elizabeth A. Sackler Center for Feminist Art at the Brooklyn Museum from 2003 to 2008, she organized several exhibitions, including the critically acclaimed *Global Feminisms*, co-curated with Linda Nochlin, and *Ghada Amer: Love Has No End*. Prior to joining the Brooklyn Museum, she taught Contemporary Art History at Tufts University, wrote art criticism for *Art in America*, and organized a number of international exhibitions, most notably *neoqueer* at the Center on Contemporary Art, Seattle. Her recent curatorial projects include *La Mirada Iracunda (The Furious Gaze)*, *Nayland Blake: Behavior*, and *Carolee Schneemann: Painting, What It Became*. Dr. Reilly received her M.A. and Ph.D. from the Institute of Fine Arts at New York University.

To find out more about Charta,
and to learn about our most recent publications, visit

www.chartaartbooks.it

Printed in April 2009
by Leva, Sesto San Giovanni
for Edizioni Charta